LABOUR MARKET AND INSTITUTION IN INDIA

1990s and Beyond

LABOUR MARKET AND INSTITUTION IN INDIA

1990s and Beyond

Edited by

SHUJI UCHIKAWA

MANOHAR
2003

First published 2003

ISBN 81-7304-486-4

Published by

Ajay Kumar Jain for
Manohar Publishers & Distributors
4753/23 Ansari Road, Daryaganj
New Delhi 110 002

Typeset at

Digigrafics
New Delhi 110 049

Printed at

Print Perfect
Delhi 110 064

Contents

Contents

Preface

Although growth rates of GDP improved after economic reforms in 1991, Indian economy has faced recession since mid-1990s. Under the recession, amendment of labour law became an issue. There is an argument that rigidity of labour market prevents growth of investment and employment. It is argued not only in India but also Japan. Indian labour law might be relatively strict, compared with other developing countries. It is not clear, however, how labour law and other institution has restricted growth of employment.

This project tries to examine the effects of economic reforms on labour market and institution. We have investigated the trends of employments and labour productivity to identify effects of economic reforms. As labour market is heterogeneous, each author focuses on different aspects.

This volume is originally published as *Labour Market and Institution in India: 1990s and Beyond* (ASEDP 63) from Institute of Developing Economies-Japan External Trade Organization (IDE-JETRO).

Mumbai SHUJI UCHIKAWA
15 March 2002

Introduction

After economic reforms, circumstances of Indian economy changed. As industrial licensing was withdrawn, companies could expand capacity and set up new units on the basis of their own judgement. In fact, investment in industry grew rapidly after 1991. Regulation on financial sector was also relaxed. Imports increased because quantitative regulations on imports were abolished and import duty has been reduced. Domestic and foreign companies in India were exposed to severe competition. They are forced to adjust to new circumstances. On the other hand, India still has serious poverty. Seventy-four per cent population was living in rural area in 2001. The unorganized sector in urban and rural area is absorbing employment. Many populations are working in unorganized sector, living below and just above poverty line.

The purpose of this study is to examine change of institution in labour market after economic reforms. Labour market is different from other markets in role of institution. Institution plays an important role in labour market. At macro level, not only labour laws and trade unions but also subcontracting affect market. At micro level, wage of employees depends on recruitment and promotion system and labour management. Economic reforms had different impacts on industries and sectors. Each author focuses on the organized sector, the unorganized sector, the financial sector, declining industries and subcontracting.

R.C. Datta emphasizes the role of institution in labour market. He finds out that institutions evolved in the internal labour market of a unionized firm do not supersede the market forces in the determination of wage differential among firm's workers. External and internal labour market institutions are primarily concerned with fairness in the distribution of workload and wages, within the non-market framework of the employment relation.

Shuji Uchikawa examines employments of the organized sector. It was argued that labour market rigidities caused by government regulation of wages and job securities restrict expansion of employment opportunities. He tried to refute it. Medium scale units employing 50 to 199 gained employment during the 1980s and 1990s. As worker number per unit did not changed in most of industries, it seems that disparities of gross profit ratio did not arise as a result of differences of employment size within the same industry. It was caused by change of industrial structure.

Jeemol Unni compares growth rates of GDP, employment and labour productivity between the organized and unorganized sectors. She argues a dynamic element was introduced in the economy with reforms in an effort to achieve more flexibility in the system. The introduction of flexibility in the labour market led to some displacement of labour and an informalization of the labour force. Although some positive linkages were observed between two sectors, there was an increase in differentials in labour productivity and earnings indicating labour market conditions in the economy as a whole.

Errol D'souza compared turnover per employee of the public sector banks and that of the private and foreign banks. Private banks improved turnover per employee much faster than public sector banks in the 1990s. He ascribed the reason to downsizing of the clerical and subordinate cadres in the private and foreign banks. The composition of the workforce in public sector banks by contrast is still dominates by the clerical and subordinate staffs. Moreover, he argues an internal labour market followed by the public sector bank is not appropriate to run organization efficiently and discourages the motivation of employees.

Tirthankar Roy points out that the overall extent of job-loss in the organized sector was limited in the 1990s. The problems of firm-bankruptcy and loss of jobs have been especially acute in certain industries where these problems have had older roots, certain firms within these industries, the late-1990s recession and older industrialized states. He argues reallocation of labour from declining to profitable sectors took place significantly within the organized sector and between the organized and the unorganized sectors. Firms that have survived within the declining industries, aggressively pursue contract employment and plant-level bargaining.

K.V. Ramaswamy analyses the impact of outsourcing practices on labour market outcomes after economic reforms. The value of subcontracting activity was growing at a faster rate than growth rate of output in organized manufacturing during the 1990s. If enterprises contract out exclusively with the objective of saving labour costs, the growth of contracting should result in greater earnings inequalities between the organized and the unorganized sectors. There is no evidence of widening of real earnings differentials among the two sectors. Moreover, negative effects are not observed in terms of earning per worker and employment in the unorganized sector of contract intensive industries.

SHUJI UCHIKAWA

Labour Market—Social Institution, Economic Reforms and Social Cost

R.C. DATTA

INTRODUCTION

Within the dominant neoclassical paradigm of labour economics, labour market is defined as one where there are demanders and suppliers, who engage in trade of labour, like they do for any other product or factor of production. Because labour has a price—wage, the supply and demand of labour are likened to exchange on a market. The theory envisions rational workers as sellers and employers as buyers, of labour, coming together in a competitive market in which their mutual exchange decisions yield an equilibrium wage rate and an equilibrium level of employment. With various assumptions about human behaviour including individuals as Utility Maximizers individualists who have the cognitive ability to exercise rational choice, the theory developed the model of economic man who is powerful enough to calculate the value of alternative outcomes to make optimal choice.

A strict interpretation of this theory evokes the notion of an auction market in which workers are openly and continuously competing for jobs and firms are persistently bidding to attract hire and retain labour services. It is assumed by the orthodox theory that the *firm* as an *institution* does not pose any obstacle to the competitive pressures of the labour market and thus the 'prices' of the labour, i.e. the wage rates of every type of labour employed by the firm are set right by the market forces.

Many scholars have repeatedly found this portrayal of the labour market sorely at the odds with the real world, especially the institu-

*This paper has benefited from discussions and comments from Errol D'Souza.

tionalists. Probably that is the reason why Samuelson (1951) noted the difficulties in applying standard neoclassical economic analysis to the employment relationship, and mentioned,

> . . . I fear that when the economic theorist turns to the problem of wage determination and labour economics, his voice becomes muted and his speech halting. If he is honest with himself, he must confess to a tremendous amount of uncertainty and self doubt concerning even the most basic and elementary parts of the subject.

Employment relation is not just a market-mediated exchange where price of labour is calculated as if it is a 'dead fish'.

Labour Market transactions do deviate from transactions in commodity markets. Because workers appear in the labour markets as subjects as well as objects, both market and non-market aspects of employment relations are viewed as important and the exchange takes place in two distinct stages: immediate market transactions, i.e. hiring of labour, and actual exchange, i.e. conversion of hired 'raw labour' (Pencavel 1991) into effective labour in the production process. Once the hiring process is made, the market dimension of the transaction in employment relation becomes less important and a non-market non-wage attributes of the labour market transactions including authority relation becomes very important. Supply of effort, willingness to adjust, quality of work performed, development of skills, knowledge about production processes and social technology, all depends on how workers perceive their situation. The employment arrangement with informational asymmetries and the temporal nature of exchange along with dignity, mutual respect and social relations are key notions to understand the labour market relations. This is the reason why Stiglitz (2000) says,

> Labour is not like other factors. Workers have to be motivated to perform. While under some circumstances, it may be difficult to coach a machine to behave in the way desired (e.g., trying to get a computer not to crash), what is entailed in eliciting the desired behaviour out of a person and out of a machine are, I would argue, fundamentally different.

And according to Solow (1980), the failure of labour markets to clear can be attributed to 'social conventions, or principles of behaviour, whose source is not entirely individualistic'. He has further commented on the importance of social values in the labour market:

> Economic man is a social, not a physiological, category. There are activities in our culture in which it is socially acceptable and expected that individual pecuniary self-interest will be the overriding decision criterion: Choosing a portfolio of securities, for example. There are others in which it is not: choosing a mate, for example. The labour market is more complicated than either, of course, and contains elements of both.

Most often the so-called 'distorting' LM institutions originate from above-mentioned types of market failures and are primarily intended to protect workers as subjects and not get treated purely as objects. These institutions are not constraints in the usual neoclassical sense because they are largely endogenous. Furthermore, these institutions have been responsible for structuring the labour markets. The allocation of labour within the firm, the way it is used in the production process and rewarded, the very purchase of labour time, are all affected by a much more complex system of relationships involving not just a wage in return for a number of hours worked, but also extent of worker's initiative, commitment, motivation, pride in work, loyalty, work intensity, autonomy in determining pace and content of work, work environment, a social position, an income level and set of consumption standards, etc. One's understanding of these complex relationships makes it clear how important it is to distinguish the human factor of production, labour, and other factors which are used in cooperation with labour in the productive process.

> Labour is subject to complex social and psychological forces. People are less receptive to direction than a piece of equipment. They react to their environment. . . . In their working environment, they are not individuals but form part of a group, open to group pressures and values. The place of work is not merely part of an economic process but also a social institution. And so is the labour market. In such a context, people develop norms about what is right and wrong and fair. Work is not merely to earn an income. It has a meaning in itself. The size of payment for work reflects on the worth, status and self-esteem of the person concerned. People measure their worth not in absolute terms but relative to one another. But while the financial incentive is important, people are also motivated by non-financial considerations. (Issac 1992)

It is within this framework psychological contract between firms and workers gets implicitly established, workers give a gift to the firm in the form of a level of effort above the firm's work rule. This gift is motivated by the workers' sentiment for each other and their sentiments for the firm. The workers expect that the firm will reciprocate their gift through the payment of fair wages, since the giving of gifts is codified in terms of norms of behaviour, which imposes reciprocity (Akerlof 1982).

Because of these non-economic aspects of employment relations a wide range of institutions both internal and external, formal and informal, evolve in the labour market which are concerned not just with efficiency but also with the distribution and control aspect of labour market, conspicuously missing in neoclassical treatment of the subject. The labour institutions are defined as rules, procedures, policies, organization and work practices, while making use of labour in the production process. These institutions are set both internally in an enterprise and also externally as labour legislation. These institutions are projected as 'irrational' behaviour reflecting 'rigidities', 'imperfections' and 'distortions' in the labour market and often alleged in the recent years of globalization, inimical to flexibility in labour market, productivity growth, and employment expansion.

It is within the above-mentioned framework that we will make an attempt to look inside the functioning of some of the aspects of labour markets in India.

The objectives are:

(a) To understand internal labour market functioning as an institution and to test its efficiency in a neoclassical human capital theoretical framework.
(b) To make an attempt to show that labour markets are not as 'rigid' as has been 'alleged' by the advocates of labour market reforms.
(c) To attempt demonstrating and measuring the social cost that displaced workers have experienced resulting from their job losses during the reform period.

The basic institutional framework within which most medium and large size manufacturing sector firms, especially the ones employing 100 or more workers in the production process, work is provided by several legal enactments dealing with employment, working conditions, social security, labour relations and labour welfare. Many of these, especially the large one do develop internal labour market characteristics.

INTERNAL LABOUR MARKET AS AN INSTITUTION

Internal labour market is defined as an administrative unit, such as a plant, office, or other employing bodies, within which the pricing and allocation of labour are determined primarily by a set of prescribed rules and procedures rather than by impersonal market forces. Within many firms in the structured organized labour market, we find more or less elaborate hierarchies of jobs, each of which centres upon certain tasks and skills. The structure of jobs and movement on the job ladder is determined by the rules and processes, which are typically designed by conscious human decisions. A new worker will typically enter at the bottom level of the job ladder and the position is called a 'port of entry'. The institutionalization of the labour market is reflected in all sorts of 'work practices' on which agreements are signed in hundreds of firms between the parties involving employers, unions as well as governments.

For example, in an engineering manufacturing company the workmen are classified by designations like setter, machinist, fabricator, surface treater, winder, electrician, welder, assembler, mechanic, checker/inspector, etc., in 8 job levels with top level job—the 9th, without any designation. There are group leaders classified in the 4 job levels. The job level descriptions applicable to all the job levels are defined by the industrial engineering department, many a times with Union's unit head participating and negotiating the tasks, skill level required and workload implied. This lays down the attributes required for performing the jobs in each job level. The attributes mainly cover knowledge, skill, learning/experience period, trade, initiative, etc. A smooth flow of work and opportunities for the workmen to learn various skills and to move up in the hierarchy on the job ladder is also formally written down in the agreement. The flexibility of deployment within a business division is also negotiated with the union of workers and the workers become eligible for 'multiskill' allowance.

This institutionalization of work practices diminishes the role of market forces as determinants of wages and employment. Does it mean the market forces are superseded by the administrative rules, procedures, and work practices? Or are the administrative rules, procedures and work practices act only as a veil? Are these practices at odds with allocative efficiency? Can one justify these because of their dynamic efficiency elements?

METHODOLOGY

The theoretical model that we have employed in order to answer some of these questions is recursive, and implicit in its nature are the following set of equations:

$$P = a_o + a_1 Ed + a_2 Ex + A_3 Ft + U_1, \quad (1)$$

$$Y = b_o + b_1 Ed + b_2 Ex + U_2 \quad (2)$$

$$Y = c_o + C_1 Ed + C_2 Ex + C_3 P \quad (3)$$

where P = Performance Rating
Ed = Formal education in years
Ex = Work experience (Age-Ed-6)
Ft = Formal training at the Training Centre. Used as Dummy Variable Ft = 1 and NOFT = 0.
Y = Gross earning per annum.
U_1, U_2 and U_3 are the residuals in the respective equations.

The postulated relationships are assumed to be linear and may be correctly estimated by utilizing ordinary least square regression technique to each of the equations. The model, however, will be expanded to allow for diminishing marginal effects of some variables (Mincer 1974).

All this data are taken from the personal files of the employees of a single firm.

RESULTS AND ANALYSIS

The empirical results presented in this paper are based exclusively on a population of 1802 male full-time workers working in one of the large multinational engineering firms in the Indian private sector.

The data are taken from the computerized file of their personal records.

TABLE 1. MEANS AND STANDARD DEVIATIONS IN THE SAMPLE

Variable	*Mean*	*S.D.*
Ed	8.520	2.593
Y	55,376.407	15,877.769
P	15.760	2.960
Ex	17.343	6.289
Ex^2	340.323	239.378
Ft	.094	.293

TABLE 2. CORRELATION MATRIX

	Ed	*P*	*Ft*	*Ex*	*Ex²*	*LogY*
Ed	1.000	.119	.184	-.203	-.231	-.016
P		1.000	.168	.149	.140	.356
Ft			1.000	-.243	-.236	0.580
Ex				1.000	.972	.668
Ex^2					1.000	.631
LogY						1.000

Table 1 gives the means and standard deviations of the all major variables appearing in the sample.

In Table 2 we have presented the correlation matrix for all the variables which entered our earnings and performance functions, given by the recursive model. Ex^2 term have been introduced to account for the observed Mincerian parabolic experience-earnings profiles.

Typical Earnings Function

In Table 3 we have shown the results of typical Mincerian earnings function. In it is seen that formal schooling and experience explain

TABLE 3. MINCERIAN EARNINGS FUNCTION

Log Y = f (Ed, Ex, Ex²)	
Variable	*Coefficient*
Ed	.008 (7.287)
Ex	.026 (14.489)
Ex^2	-.001 (-4.001)
Constant	10.489
R^2	.464
F-value	658.990

't' statistics in parenthesis

about 46 per cent of the dispersion of earnings. Regression coefficients of both schooling and experience are statistically significant.

Every additional year of formal education adds 0.8 per cent into the annual earnings of a worker. Every year of on-the-job experience yield an increase of 2.6 per cent of a worker's annual earnings. A significantly negative coefficient of Ex^2 exhibit a clearly defined parabola.

PERFORMANCE FUNCTION

The performance on the job of workers in this firm is rated every year by the management. Various factors which are considered while giving rating on a scale of 1 to 40 are output, quality of work (rejection, etc.), ability to do variety of jobs, orderliness and cleanliness, punctuality of work, care of tools and machinery and attendance record. On the basis of these ratings, future training needs of workers are identified.

We have regressed performance ratings of workers on typical human capital variables, i.e. schooling and experience. The results are shown in Table 4.

Although both the human capital variables are significant but the model explains only 3.5 per cent of the variation in job performances of workers.

However, when we included in the in-firm-training as additional variable in the 'performance function' the explanatory power of the model changed. The results are shown in Table 5.

Formal education has lost its significance in the presence of in-firm-training in determining one's performance on the job. On the

TABLE 4. PERFORMANCE FUNCTION I

$P = f(Ed, Ex)$

Variable	*Coefficient*
Ed	.175 (5.76)
Ex	.071 (6.07)
Constant	13.147
R^2	.035
F-value	28.900

't' statistics in parenthesis

TABLE 5. PERFORMANCE FUNCTION II

P = f (Ed, Ex, Ft)	
Variable	*Coefficient*
Ed	.017 (.842)
Ex	.048 (5.692)
Ft	.968 (5.281)
Constant	6.033
R^2	.474
F-value	323.700

't' statistics in parenthesis

job experience is significant and a year of it adds .04 unit in the worker's performance rating. Ft is also significant in determining on the job performance. Those with Ft gains almost a unit increase in their performance rating.

Most significantly the explanatory power of the model goes up to 47 per cent and which is a little more than the explanatory power of typical human capital variables in the earnings function in Table 3.

In our next equation we have added the in-firm-training as a variable in Mincerian earnings function. The results (Table 6) shows that all the variables are statistically significant and the model explains 49 per cent of variation in earnings. Those with in-firm-training increase their annual earnings by almost 10 per cent compared to 2.8 per cent and .5 per cent contribution of an additional year of on-the-job experience and an additional year of formal education, respectively.

At this point, we would like to mention that Nelson and Phelps (1966) viewed in their work that more educated workers are able to adjust to disequilibria. Their view has been further developed by

TABLE 6. EXPANDED EARNINGS FUNCTION

Log Y = f (Ed, Ft, Ex, Ex^2)	
Variable	*Coefficient*
Ed	.005 (4.951)
Ft	.098 (10.457)
Ex	.028 (15.968)
Ex^2	-.002 (-4.83)
Constant	568.54
R^2	.493
F-value	443.220

Welch (1970) and in its most general form by Schultz (1975). It seems in-firm-training of the workers enable them adapt more quickly to the dynamic environment. Off-the-job conceptual training on attitude building, team building, statistical process control, on computer numerically controlled machines, techniques of total quality management, and ISO 9000, are a few examples of such continuous in-firm-training to upgrade quality of human capital to deal with competitive environment.

So our typical Human Capital Model explains almost 50 per cent of the earnings variation within a firm among workers, which indicates that the internal labour market is quite efficient within the institutional framework of equity and fairness. Researchers (Fogel 1982) in the field of industrial relations have shown that in addition to contributing towards productivity, with longer years of service with the firm, workers do develop a growing equity position or a sort of property right in their job. As a matter of fairness within a psychological contract framework, therefore, it is believed that earnings and movement up the job ladder results with increase in seniority. An equity and fairness in the individual earnings differentials is maintained by many firms through institutions like compa ratio in order to achieve optimality of efficiency and to work as a team.

CAUSES OF INDUSTRIAL DISPUTES

In the second stage of our analysis of Labour Market as a Social Institution, we have attempted looking into the secondary data on industrial disputes in India classified by causes over the years.

The data in Table 7 clearly shows that never since 1991 till 1999 not more than about one-third of the aggregated industrial disputes have been caused by 'wage' related issues. The so-called common answer that the workers are utility maximizer individualists looking for more money is not necessarily true. Almost equal percentage of disputes during this period are because of interpersonal relations—social relations?

As we have mentioned in the introductory section, the second stage of labour exchange deals with conversion of 'raw' labour into effective actual work effort that take place within an authority relation framework where the 'price' of labour is less important issue and social relations dominates.

LABOUR INSTITUTIONS AND REFORMS IN INDIA

One of the key aspects of the structural adjustment programme, initiated in India in the wake of globalizing India's economy, has been towards the improvement in the 'efficiency' in the labour market functioning. It has been argued that the labour productivity in India is very low and this along with 'rigidities' created by the institutional framework within which labour market works are significantly responsible for the 'uncompetitiveness' of the Indian industry in the

TABLE 7. PERCENTAGE DISTRIBUTION OF INDUSTRIAL DISPUTE CLASSIFIED BY CAUSES OVER YEARS

Cause Groups/ Years	*1991*	*1992*	*1993*	*1994*	*1995*	*1996*	*1997*	*1998*	*1999*
Wages & Allowances	24.0	22.6	26.0	29.5	30.0	24.4	23.4	21.2	21.30
Bonus	3.9	7.8	6.7	7.7	7.4	8.2	8.6	11.2	1.60
Personnel & Retrenchment	17.0	17.2	19.7	17.7	19.2	19.2	20.5	16.7	18.90
Leave & Hours of Work/Shift working	1.0	1.6	1.7	1.4	2.0	1.8	2.4	1.3	1.60
Indiscipline & Violence	18.5	21.8	19.6	16.9	14.9	18.2	19.9	21.1	19.68
Others	16.6	14.1	11.7	9.8	5.4	7.3	6.5	8.1	9.45
Not known	2.1	1.9	2.9	1.7	2.7	4.0	2.8	4.5	2.36
Lay-off	0.2	0.3	0.1	0.2	0.4	0.3	0.5	0.6	0.78
Inter/Intra Union Rivalry	0.3	0.8	1.4	0.8	0.7	1.0	0.9	0.6	0.78
Gherao	0.1	0.1	0.1	0.1	0.1	–	–	–	–
Non Implementation or in connection with Labour Enactment, Labour Awards & Labour Agreements	0.6	0.6	2.1	3.1	4.0	4.2	3.3	29.0	1.6
Charter of Demands	7.0	4.5	2.4	4.6	5.7	6.1	5.2	8.8	0.78
Workload	0.3	0.9	0.6	0.8	0.9	0.5	0.7	0.6	–
Surplus Labour	0.1	0.1	0.1	0.1	–	0.1	0.1	–	–
Betterment of Amenities	1.7	1.8	0.9	1.3	1.7	1.8	2.6	1.1	4.72
Suspensions/Change of Manufacturing Process	0.2	0.1	0.1	0.1	–	0.1	–	0.1	–
Standing Orders/ Rules/Service Conditions/Safety Measures	6.4	3.8	3.9	4.2	4.9	2.8	2.6	1.2	16.53

SOURCE: Ministry of Labour, *Labour Statistics*, various issues.

international markets. Thus, a drastic rehauling of the labour market policies and institutions have been officially advocated by the policy-makers. More specifically, external legal labour institutions like Industrial Disputes Act, 1947, Trade Unions Act, 1926, Contract Labour (Regulation and Abolition) Act, 1970, among others have been under attack by the employers and the government. However, worker's unions believe dilution of these acts will bring in hire and fire policy. The employer and the government have also been seeing these laws as the biggest impediments to the creation of *quality employment* in India.

Labour market in India has been alleged as 'rigid' and 'restraining' expansion of employment in the organized sector primarily due to the nature of our labour laws. These labour laws must be reformed, made flexible, it has been argued, to make Indian industry domestically and internationally competitive, to encourage production of labour-intensive products with higher 'elasticities' of employment, and thus expand 'quality' employment. In a recent study of Planning Commission (2001) on employment opportunities in India, it has been stated that,

> . . . if the minimum wage fixed by law is too high, it raises the cost of labour intensive activities and products in the organised sector (which is where the laws are enforced) relative to other products and activities and relative to the same products produced in the unorganised sector where the law cannot be enforced. Employers in the organised sector will tend to shift to more capital-intensive activities and products which implies that minimum wages may be effectively raised in the organised sector, but at the cost of lower level of employment than would exist otherwise in these products in the organised sector. Similarly, laws designed to provide security of employment reduce the flexibility available to employers to adjust the labour force in response to changing circumstances and employers are likely to respond by shying away from labour using activities. Additional security for existing job opportunities is therefore obtained only at the cost of expansion of employment.

So, shall we dilute the labour protection legislation which provides the rights those are termed as 'rigidities' and 'privileges' to the workers in the organized sector because the exploitative wages and working conditions of unorganized sector workers are outcompeting the former? How about enacting social security legislation for the unorganized labour? Have textile mills in organized sector gone for rotor spinning or airjet looms to save on labour? Have engineering firms installed micro-electronics based capital-intensive computer numerically controlled machines to save on labour and labour laws? Is the use of Badli workers in textile mills or that of contract workers, not a form of number flexibility? Is the only relatively (relative to decentralized sector) high labour cost making these mills uncompetitive? How about high cost of power? Cost of water? The political economy of the land itself ?

The real world it seems is different. The data indicate that the capital-labour ratio in manufacturing sector has been increasing and especially in the years following the reform, it has doubled. In addition to this, the sectors, which traditionally had high labour content in the product, are either declining or are becoming both physical and human capital-intensive resulting in situation of jobless growth. Furthermore, I would like to mention the adoption of capital-intensive technology rather than labour-intensive one is *not* necessarily a conscious decision on the part of employer in order *not to hire* human being, a worker, as he is going to get stuck with him due to these so-called 'rigid' labour laws. According to my understanding an Airjet loom is not bought by a composite textile mill in order to save on labour—the 'hassle' factor of production and to circumvent the 'rigid' legislation. A CNC machine is not introduced on the shopfloor to save labour. These technologies produce goods of better quality, variety and precision and many a time for different market segments. Furthermore, it is very difficult to accept that these capital-intensive technologies will not be used and employers will start using labour in production methods if the so-called 'rigid' labour laws are diluted. It can further be added here that the production relation in a typical firm in India, in the organized sector is characterized by tall hierarchical structure with minimal employee participation thus conforming to the resistance oriented Taylorist model. All those firms and nations which are internationally competitive have made consciously significant departure from such models independent of external structural constraints or changes. This is the fundamental of 'labour market flexibility' which is typically 'internal' and 'attitudinal' that determines the competitiveness of a firm. What our policy-makers are attempting to do in this regard are mostly peripheral.

In fact, firms at plant level have been able to achieve the functional flexibility related to multi-tasking, multi-skilling, and multi-machine operations. Textile mills in their loom sheds have shifted from strict division of labour between weaver and batteryfiller to weaver-cum-batteryfiller by negotiating with the unions over the resulting workload content within a framework of so-called 'rigid' labour laws. The labour redundancy arising out of such 'achievement' of functional flexibility is dealt with by introducing an early 'voluntary' separation scheme for the workers. What happen to them during the post-early 'voluntary' retirement phase is a separate story.

Employers have also been able to negotiate the numerical and wage flexibility at plant levels in many firms in recent years. The detail data related to these of a large firm with several manufacturing plants is given in Table 8 and Figure 1 and is self-explanatory. We would like to call these temporary as regular-temporaries as every

TABLE 8. WAGE FLEXIBILITY: TEMPORARY *vs*. PERMANENT WORKMEN

(*Rs. per month*)

	GRADE 'A'		*GRADE 'B'*		*GRADE 'C'*	
	Temporary	*Permanent*	*Temporary*	*Permanent*	*Temporary*	*Permanent*
	Old	*Old*	*Old*	*Old*	*Old*	*Old*
Total	5,563.00	5,563.00	5,571.00	5,571.00	5,586.00	5,586.00
Gross Wages	6,171.15	8,431.20	6,179.60	8,439.60	6,195.30	8,455.30
Cost to Company	7,046.96	10,239.00	7,056.30	10,248.00	7,073.90	10,269.00

(Year 2000)

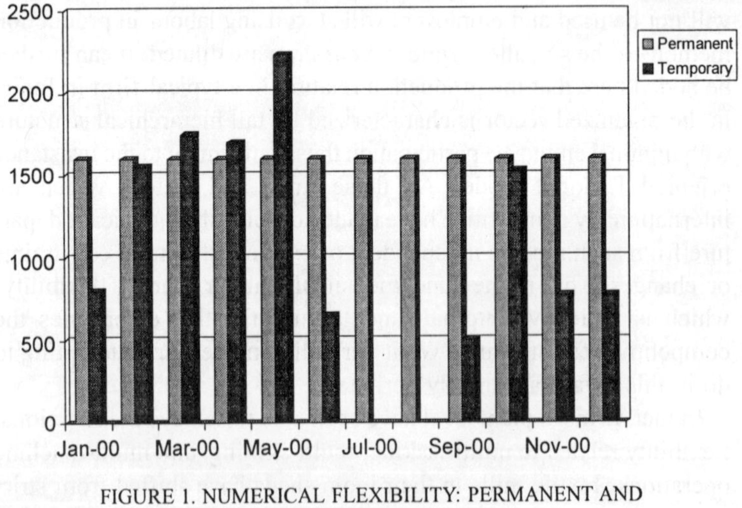

FIGURE 1. NUMERICAL FLEXIBILITY: PERMANENT AND TEMPORARY WORKMEN

year with a gap of 2-3 months the same individual comes back to work on the shop-floor. They are as much 'skilled' for the work as the permanent ones. The firms have been using this type of arrangement over the past many years and have gained the benefits of functional, wage, and numerical flexibilities.

What is still demanded by our typical employers and is supported by our policy-makers relates to 'hire and fire' dimension of labour market flexibility and that too without taking any social responsibility towards ones losing jobs. More specifically the following labour laws are identified to be diluted.

INDUSTRIAL DISPUTES ACT, 1947 AND CONTRACT LABOUR (ABOLITION AND REGULATION) ACT (1970)

Under the Industrial Disputes Act (1947) in Chapter V(b) any retrenchment (Section 25N), lay-off (Section 25M) or closure (Section 25O) of an industrial set-up having employed more than 100 workers is required to take prior permission from the appropriate government. The penalty for lay-off (Section 25Q), retrenchment (Section 25Q) or closure (Section 25R) without government permission can lead to a prison sentence and a fine for the employer. If still an employer closes down the unit even after refusal by the appropriate authorities, he can be imprisoned up to one year or fined up to Rs. 5,000 or both. The law does make an exception for retrenchment resulting from power shortage or natural disaster. Furthermore, when a workman with more than 240 days service in a year is laid off, he is entitled for a compensation equal to 50 per cent of his total basic wage and dearness allowance that would have been payable to him had he not been laid off, *subject to a maximum of 45 days* (Section 25C). In the event of retrenchment the same worker is entitled to one month notice in writing, stating reasons for retrenchment and 15 days' compensation for each year of service at 50 per cent of basic wages plus dearness allowance (Section 25F). In case of closure of unit, workmen who have completed not less than one year of continuous service in the undertaking are entitled to notice and compensation in accordance with the provision of Section 25F (Section 25FFF).

The fact is, even if the government refuses permission for lay-off and retrenchment of workers or closure of a unit, employers still somehow manage to close down, lay-off and retrench workers for

TABLE 9. DISPLACEMENT OF WORKERS AND LABOUR LAWS

Year	*No. of units affecting closure*	*No. of workers affected*	*No. of units affecting lay-off*	*No. of workers laid-off*	*No. of units affecting retrench-ment*	*No. of workers retren-ched*	*Total no. of workers affected*
1976	NA	NA	1,663	2,05,370	1,049	24,417	26,080
1977	871	96,311	1,566	2,93,265	732	16,262	4,05,838
1978	332	13,665	1,304	2,46,424	745	23,049	2,83,138
1979	337	18,722	1,621	3,50,529	741	17,841	3,87,092
1980	338	18,052	1,610	3,04,090	724	15,341	3,37,483
1981	349	37,377	1,318	3,07,812	725	17,314	3,62,503
1982	286	26,602	1,556	3,02,607	754	15,469	3,44,678
1983	226	43,234	1,319	2,41,217	734	21,233	3,05,684
1984	188	71,937	901	1,49,135	579	11,082	2,32,154
1985	203	31,268	732	1,05,774	453	11,280	1,48,322
1986	236	28,027	828	1,32,275	480	9,164	1,69,466
1987	198	19,149	709	1,44,925	356	4,520	1,68,594
1988	259	14,086	587	1,05,109	379	4,904	1,24,099
1989	251	7,190	554	71,290	181	3,291	81,771
1990	167	7,923	456	65,560	269	3,038	76,521
1991	238	21,439	461	71,060	235	4,396	96,895
1992	187	12,422	477	1,07,612	222	3,836	1,23,870
1993	493	25,658	425	65,628	189	2,891	94,177
1994	228	21,394	342	58,067	135	2,192	81,653
1995	183	14,495	284	61,986	94	1,792	78,273
1996	204	11,390	307	61,337	79	2,372	75,099
1997	154	12,944	307	65,165	161	3,242	81,351
1998	175	13,386	294	45,243	135	2,030	60,659
1999	159	15,707	239	33,710	176	2,503	51,920
2000	136	11,796	208	37,061	109	2,963	51,820

NOTES: Figures for the year 1978, 1979 and 1980 is provisional for lay-off and retrenchment.
Figures for the year 1999 and 2000 is provisional.
NA: Not Available.

SOURCE: Ministry of Labour, *Annual Review on Closure, Retrenchment & Lay-offs*, various years.

which it does not mind paying a meagre few hundred rupees as a fine. The data in the Table 9 clearly shows how these barriers to exit of workers and units are largely illusory and industry has been managing before and after the reforms to cross these barriers to exit without much of a problem.

We would like to add here that the early separation schemes in the last one decade in the Indian industry, both in private and public sector, have already made many of these sections under the Industrial Disputes Act (1947) partly redundant.

There is one Section 9A which requires a Notice of Change to be given to the workmen who are likely to get affected including retrenchment, by introduction of any new technology or change in nature of work due to new work practices, which is also under attack for its deletion because it is felt that this has been coming in the way of introduction of flexible practices which are required to become competitive. In the recent years, we have rarely come across a major conflict arising because of Section 9A in the industry. However, wherever it has arisen, it is primarily due to the threat, which a worker faces to be retrenched, or because of one's inability of being retrainable in getting redeployed.

Another labour legislation alleged to have become obstacle in making labour market more efficient is The Contract Labour (Regulation and Abolition) Act of 1970 that was enacted to regulate the practice of contract labour. The real intent of this legislation was to eliminate the exploitative wages and working conditions of the contract workers by providing them with basic equitable social security and also to limit the free play of market forces in the labour market where the factor of production is not an inanimated one. Here, the relationship cannot be best modelled as a market-mediated exchange. Such a model is incomplete as it involves only the hiring of what Pancavel (1991) has termed 'raw labour'. The conversion of this raw labour—the capacity to work, into effective labour, or actual work effort is a function of working conditions. These working conditions are mostly neglected by the employers while hiring contract labour under '*sham contracts*' which is why the Act makes the labour market perceived as 'rigid'. A causal link running from the general well-being of workers to their workplace performance has been very well established under efficiency wage theory.

The fact is contractualization in the labour market is increasing, and it is aiding labour markets becoming flexible, but, whether that has made product market and labour market efficient, is still not known.

In addition to above-mentioned 'regular' exit, retrenchment, and contractualization of labour in the organized industrial sector, industrial restructuring under the reforms has resulted in redundancy and displacement of workers both in private and public sector enterprises. Similar adverse affects have been witnessed in almost all the countries of Latin America and that of South and South-East

TABLE 10. REDUNDANCY ARISING FROM PRIVATIZATION IN SOUTH ASIA

Country	*PSE Employment*	*Redundancy (%)*
Bangladesh	240 thousand	25
India	9.8 million	23
Nepal	46.7 thousand	60
Pakistan	34.6 thousand	63
Sri Lanka	120 thousand	53

SOURCE: Joshi (2000).

Asia which adopted stabilization and Structural Adjustment Programmes.

A recent study of five South Asian countries on 'Privatization in South Asia' has shown these adverse effects on the labour market in the form of millions of employees of the public sector becoming redundant resulting from the privatization policies under the reforms. We have reproduced these figures in the Table 10.

Restructuring and privatization processes in India has resulted in thousands of job losses in the recent years of economic reforms. Typically early 'voluntary' separation schemes are introduced to reduce the resistance of organized labour and thus make sale of unit more attractive for the bidders. However, once the unit is privatized, a 'no-retrenchment' clause in the sale agreement is included to be binding on the buyer for a certain time period. After the merger or acquisition, once various new performance enhancing work practices are introduced, many workers become redundant leading to introduction of another early 'voluntary' retirement scheme and job losses. Typical firm behaviour is shown in Figures 2 and 3.

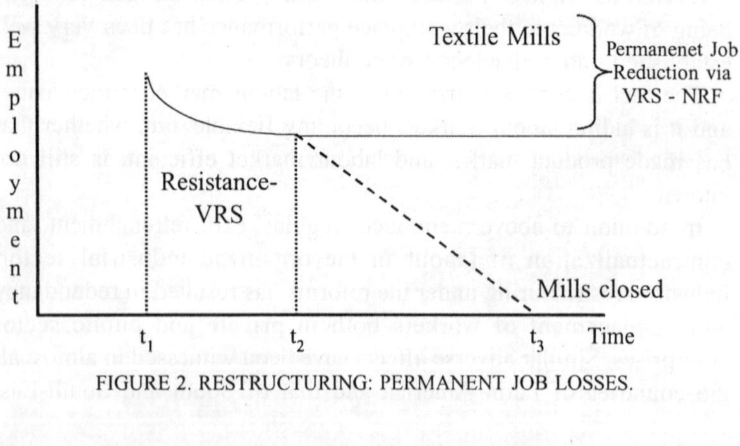

FIGURE 2. RESTRUCTURING: PERMANENT JOB LOSSES.

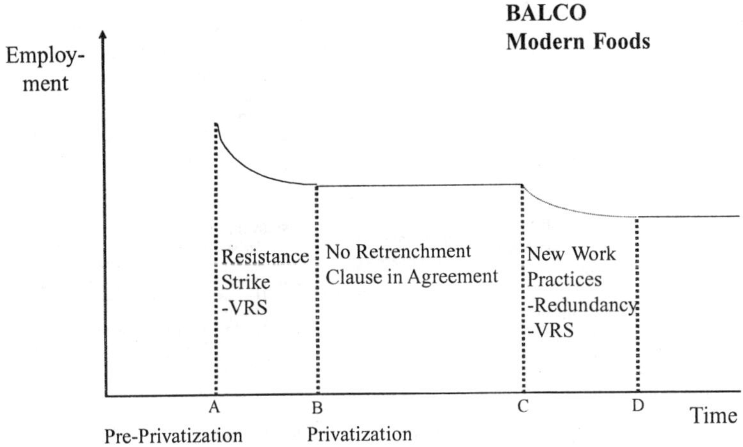

FIGURE 3. PRIVATIZATION AND JOB LOSSES.

SOCIAL COSTS OF REFORMS

Economic reforms have certainly aggravated the problems through restructuring, privatization, modernization, downsizing and labour market reforms have increased the social cost of adjustment vis-à-vis economic benefits. This has also been observed that the negative control of labour costs, many a time, is pursued simply to restore profitability by retrenching workers without becoming competitive or generating any underlying improvement in performance. The redundant workers, in the jargon of neoclassical economics, become labour market 'lemons'—asymmetry of information makes employers infer that all redundant workers are of low quality.

For these very reasons the policy-makers in all the countries, where Stabilization and Structural Adjustment Programmes have been implemented, expressed concern about the redundancy arising during industrial restructuring, primarily, because the job loss involves substantial economic and non-wage social-psychological costs for the adversely affected worker and his/her family. We have attempted putting job loss effects for a typical worker in the following diagram (Figure 4).

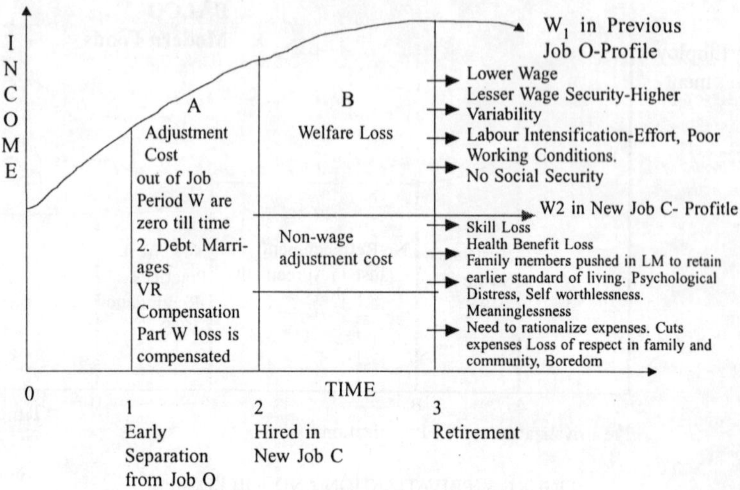

FIGURE 4. SOCIAL COSTS OF JOB LOSS FOR A WORKER.

Area A represent the adjustment cost incurred by the worker during the time period of separating from the existing job with W_1 wage profile and re-entering the market in a Job C with W_2 wage profile adjusted for the 'retrenchment compensation' during the period of unemployment. At a time 2 the redundant worker is hired back in the labour market in Job C which has W_2 as wage profile-typical of unorganized sector employment. The components of the gap between wage profiles W_1 and W_2 are typically attributed to the 'rent seeking behaviour' of worker in Job O disregarding the human capital acquired on-the-job and the efficiency wage arguments. In addition to this the social security losses are also important. And above all there are social and psychological costs on well-being experienced by the redundant worker and his family. A worker's internalized concept of self, which is based on one's feelings of mastery, and control over one's environment is destroyed. Welfare loss thus cannot be equated simply to decline in income in the alternative employment entered in by the displaced and time taken in job search. This is more true of the displaced workers who hold no reservation wage, who have no scope of retrainability and decent alternative work, and also where job/work search assistance does not exist for majority of 'displaced'. Thus, assessing 'welfare loss' due to the 'job loss' in the labour market that does not offer 'rehabilitation' in the real sense of term is extremely difficult.

One of the major variables indicating whether rehabilitation of the workers, has been successful or not, is their monthly income during the post-voluntary retirement phase. This also in a way is an indicator of the social cost. Even if one looks at the wages of the workers in the organized sector partly as a form of monopoly rent, that would be purely looking at the worker's wages as a cost factor. The fact is wage is not just cost, it is a productive factor as well, as has been shown under the Efficiency Wage theories. We must admit that even if that 'rent' is eliminated, it is not necessary that the savings thus generated will be shared with the society in the form of employment generation. It is very likely to be taken away by the principals. Furthermore, there are social and psychological cost of loosing one's job, especially in a country like India where there are not only no alternative 'decent' jobs available, most jobs are without any social security. Thus, workers gets pushed into the unorganized sector.

In our field survey we have come across views of many concerned people, that, implications of such an outcome of structural adjustment reforms is quite dangerous for the society. A typical textile worker in Mumbai who had started his career in the mill as a 'Badli Worker' and moved up to become permanent worker after spending years as Badli Worker, is back, many a time at the gate of the mill looking for work after 'experiences' of his post-voluntary retirement phase (Figure 5).

Table 11 puts together the earnings experience of voluntary retired workers in one of our studies on life after voluntary retirement of textile workers who re-entered the labour market after taking voluntary retirement option. Here, in our cases out of 251, 68.6 per cent that is 172 are working. In the Table 11 it is shown that only around 5 per

TABLE 11. WORKERS EARNINGS IN POST-VOLUNTARY RETIREMENT PHASE

Present earnings (Rs. per month)	(%)
Up to 1,000	59.46
1,001 - 2,000	25.70
2,001 - 3,500	8.50
3,501 - 5,000	2.61
5,001 - 7,500	1.64
7,501 - 10,000	1.40
10,001 & above	0.68

N = 172

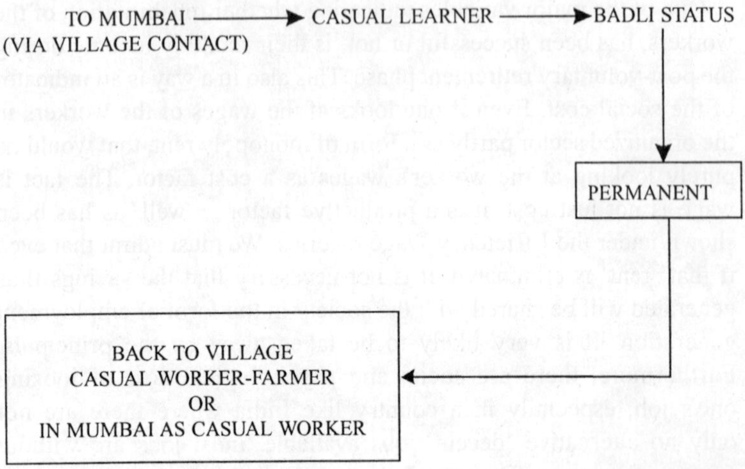

FIGURE 5. THE 'ACTUAL CYCLE OF MOBILITY' OF A TEXTILE WORKER.

cent of the textile workers have been able to earn in the market during the post-voluntary retirement phase something equivalent to their earnings before opting for VRS, i.e. around Rs. 5,000 per month. More than 85 per cent of these textile workers are making less than Rs. 2,000 per month. Very few of the workers who opted for VRS have been able to reach the income somewhat similar to as they used to get before the voluntary retirement phase.

Our findings based on our fieldwork shows that most of the workers have experienced significantly lower wages, poor working conditions, non-regular work without any basic social security, and non-monetary adjustment costs like children dropping out of schools. Most of them have spent their voluntary retirement emoluments in repaying debts and also in the marriages of their children. Literally, there has been no awareness regarding the existence of the facility of retraining under the National Renewal Fund. None of them have been given any counselling or financial investment guidance via any help-base. And finally their retraining links with the villages and land has come very handy in coping with post-retirement difficulties.

CONCLUSION

In this paper we have defined Labour Market as a Social Institution wherein employment relation is not purely a market relation, but is composed of two-stage exchange. Herein, hiring of labour is part of the incomplete exchange process that gets completed within the confines of the firm within authority relation framework which determines the degree of effective conversion of 'raw labour' hired into actual work effort. The process of conversion is embedded with formal and informal, internal and external institutions, which evolve in order to take care of efficiency, equity and distributional concerns. In the first part of paper we have used multiple regression to show that institutions evolved in the Internal Labour Market of a unionized firm do not supersede the market forces in the determination of wage differential among firm's workers. The operation of the Internal Labour Market is quite inefficient. With the help of macro data on causes of industrial conflict, we argue that external and internal Labour Market Institutions are primarily concerned with fairness in the distribution of workload and wages, within the non-market framework of the employment relation.

At the firm level it seems to us that the employers have been able to achieve numerical flexibility, wage flexibility and also the functional flexibility. The 'rigidities' of the labour legislation has not come in the way. However, the restructuring and privatization exercises have resulted in large redundancies and job losses inflicting significant social cost on the worker and his family.

REFERENCES

Akerlof, G.A., 1980, 'A Theory of Social Custom, of which Unemployment may be One Consequence', *Quarterly Journal of Economics*, 94(4), June, pp. 749-75.

———, 1982, 'Labour Contracts as Partial Gift Exchange', *Quarterly Journal of Economics*, 97(4).

Bewley, T., 1995, 'A depressed labour market index as explained by participants', *American Economic Review*, vol. 85 (Papers and Proceedings), pp. 250-4.

Blank, R. and R. Freeman, 1993, 'Evaluating the connection between social protection and economic flexibility', NBER Working Paper 4338.

Datta, R.C., 1999, A Report of Evaluation of Counselling, Retraining and Redeployment Programmes for Rationalized Workers under National Renewal Fund by Nodal Agencies set up in Mumbai, Tata Institute of Social Sciences, Mumbai.

———, 2001, *Life After Voluntary Retirement: Examining the Human Face of Structural Adjustment Program—A Field Study*, Tata Institute of Social Sciences, Mumbai.

Dow, G.K., 1996, 'Authority Relations in the Firm: Review and Agenda for Research', in John Groenewegen, ed., *Transaction Costs, Economics and Beyond*, Boston: Kluwer.

Evans-Klock, Christine et al., 1999, 'Worker Retrenchment: Preventive and Remedial Measures', *International Labour Review*, vol. 138, no.1.

Fogel, Walter, ed., 1982, *Job Equity and Other Studies in Industrial Relations: Essays in Honor of Frederic Meyers*, Los Angeles: Institute of Industrial Relations, UCLA, 1982.

Freeman, R.B. and J.L. Medoff, 1984, *What Do Unions Do?*, New York: Basic Books.

Government of India, June 2001, *Report of 'Task Force On Employment Opportunities'*, Planning Commission.

Goyal, S.K., 1999, *Privatization in India: Social Effects and Restructuring*, ILO-SAAT, New Delhi.

Hyman, R. and I. Brough, 1975, *Social Values and Industrial Relations: A Study of Fairness and Equality*, Oxford: Basil Blackwell.

Isaac, J.E., 1992a, 'Performance Related Pay: The Importance of Fairness', Working Paper No. 64, Melbourne: Centre for Industrial Relations and Labour Studies, University of Melbourne.

———, 1993, 'How Important is Industrial Relations Reform to Economic Performance?' in M. Bryce, ed., *Industrial Relations Policy Under the Microscope*, ACIRRT Working Paper No. 40, April, Sydney.

James L. Medoff and Katherine G. Abraham, 1980, 'Experience, Performance and Earnings', *Quarterly Journal of Economics*, 95, pp. 703-36.

———, 1981, 'Are Those Paid More Really More Productive: The Case of Experience', *Journal of Human Resources*, 16, pp. 188-216.

Joshi, Gopal, 2000, *Privatization in South Asia—Minimizing Negative Social Effects through Restructuring*, ILO-SAAT, New Delhi.

Levine, D.J. and L. D'Andrea-Tyson, 1990, 'Participation, Productivity and the Firm's Environment', in *Paying for Productivity: A Look at the Evidence*, ed. by A.S. Blinder, 183-243, Washington, D.C.: Brookings Institution.

Marsden, D., 1986, *The End of Economic Man? Custom and Competition in Labor Markets*, New York: St. Martin's Press.

Mehta, S.S., 1995, 'Exit Policy and Social Safety Net', *The Indian Journal of Labour Economics*, vol. 38, no. 4.

Mincer, J., 1974, *Schooling, Experience and Earnings*, National Bureau of Economic Research, USA.

Ministry of Labour, Government of India (various years), *Statistics on Closures, Retrenchments and Lay-Offs in India*, New Delhi.

Nickell, S., 1997, 'Unemployment and labour market rigidities; Europe versus North America', *Journal of Economic Perspectives*, vol. 11, pp. 55-74.

Nickell, S. and R. Layard, 1997, 'Labour market institutions and economic performance', Discussion Paper Series No. 23, Centre for Economic Performance, University of Oxford.

North, D.C., 1990, *Institutions, Institutional Change and Economic Performance*, Cambridge: Cambridge University Press.

Papola, T.S. and G. Rodgers, eds., 1992, *Labour institutions and economic development in India*, Geneva: International Institute for Labour Studies.

Patel, B.B. and Keyur Mankodi, 1998, *NRF as Safety Net in Indian Dimensions, Progress and Issues*, Gandhi Labour Institute, Ahmedabad.

Pencavel, J., 1991, *Labour Markets Under Trade Unionism*, Cambridge, Mass.: Blackwell.

Ravn, M. and J.R. Sorensen, 1997, 'Minimum Wages: Curse or Blessing?', *Research in Labour Economics*, vol. 16, pp. 343-68.

Rebitzer, J.A., 1993 'Radical Political Economy and the Economics of Labor Markets', *Journal of Economic Literature*, 31(3), September, pp. 1394-434.

Rees, A., 1993, 'The Role of Fairness in Wage Determination', *Journal of Labor Economics*, 11(1), pp. 243-52.

Ross, A.M., 1948, *Trade Union Wage Policy*, Berkeley, University of California Press.

Saint-Paul, G., 1993, 'On the political economy of labour market flexibility', *NBER Macro–economics Annual*, Cambridge, MA: MIT Press.

———, 1996, 'Exploring the political economy of labour market institutions,' *Economic Policy*, no. 23, pp. 265-300.

Samuelson, Paul, 1951, 'Economic Theory and Wages', in *The Impact of the Union*, ed. by D.M. Wright, New York: Harcourt, Brace and Company.

Solow, R., 1990, *The Labour Market as a Social Institution*, Oxford, Basil Blackwell.

———, 1980, 'On Theories of Unemployment', *American Economic Review*, 70(1).

Standing, Guy and Victor Tokman, 1991, *Towards Social Adjustment*, ILO, Geneva.

Stiglitz, Joseph, 1999, *Participation and Development: Perspectives from the Comprehensive Development Paradigm*, The World Bank.

———, 2000, *Democratic Development as the Fruits of Labour*, The World Bank.

Venkataratnam, C.S., 1992, 'Exit Policy: An Overview of Some Issues', *Indian Journal of Industrial Relations*, vol. 27, no. 4, April.

Employment in the Manufacturing Organized Sector in India: The Rise of Medium Scale Units

SHUJI UCHIKAWA

The proposition that labour market rigidities caused by government regulation of wages and job securities restrict expansion of employment opportunities depends on analysis of the manufacturing organized sector during the 1980s. In the 1980s, economic growth without increase of employment in the organized sector became an issue. P.R. Fallon and R.E.B. Lucas ascribe drop of long-run demand for employments to amendments of Industrial Disputes Act in 1976.[1] Besides, I.J. Ahluwalia and A.K. Gosh argue the sharp increase of real wage rates caused rise of the capital-labour ratio.[2] On the other hand, increase of employment in the manufacturing organized sector during the 1990s was pointed out.[3] The rise of medium scale unit employing 50-199 employees became more important in terms of employment during the 1980s and 1990s. The conditions of labour market might be reflected in the rise of medium size units. This paper examines the reasons of economic growth without increase of employment and why employment distribution shifted in favour of medium scale units.

1. TRENDS OF EMPLOYMENT IN THE ORGANIZED SECTOR

Economic reforms since 1991 induced investment boom up to 1995-6. Growth rates of gross value added (GVA) in the manufacturing organized sector improved in the first half of 1990s. Although 1991 was the turning point of macroeconomic policies, economic liberalization started in the 1980s. A comprehensive industrial policy statement was made in July 1980. In 1985 government announced the delicensing of 25 categories of industries. If liberalization in the 1980s had impact on labour market, 1991 might not have been its turning point.[4]

The organized sector includes government employees. The purpose of this paper is to analyse relationship between labour market and institution in the manufacturing sector. As supply of government service depends on political decision, government employees engaging in government service are excluded from this analysis. This paper depends on data from Annual Survey of Industries (ASI), which covers manufacturing and infrastructure, and the private and public sector units.

Since ASI does not have used-based classification, we must aggregate three digit level data to produce used-based data series. National industrial classification (NIC) was changed from 1970 code to 1987 code. After it was changed, ASI changed the classification in 1989-90 to follow new classification. This study produces used-based data series on the basis of 1987 code. GVA is deflated by chain index of industry group. Annual inflation rate of specific year, denoted by Pt, is obtained using the formula:

$$P_t = \sum \frac{WPI_{i,t}}{WPI_{i,t-1}} \frac{V_i}{V_a}$$

where Vi is net value added (NVA) of good i and Va is total NVA of the industry group. Wholesale price index of good i is compared with previous year's one and is weighted by the share of NVA in total NVA of the industry group. The index takes 1981-2 as base year.

Worker number of total industries (NIC 20-1 to 74) had grown constantly from 4.53 million in 1973-4 to 6.17 million in 1982-3 by 3.6 per cent per annum.[5] However, it fell to 5.67 million in 1986-7. Since 1986-7 it increased again by 2.7 per cent to 7.56 million in 1997-8. Table 1 shows employment decreased in many industries between 1982-3 and 1986-7. Particularly in food industry employment went down by 6.1 per sent during the period. We divide period under examination into three periods: (1) 1973-4 to 1982-3, (2) 1982-3 to 1986-7, (3) 1986-7 to 1997-8. It seems that macro economy might have affected employment in the organized sector during the second period. On the other hand, annual GVA growth rate of total industries rose from 5.0 per cent during the first and the second period and 9.4 per cent during the third period.

TABLE 1. GROWTH RATES OF GVA AND WORKER NUMBER

(%)

NIC	*GVA at 1981-2 prices*			*Number of workers*		
	I	*II*	*III*	*I*	*II*	*III*
20-1	5.8	4.5*	7.6	5.3	-6.1	2.6
22	2.3	8.0*	6.8	9.6	-5.6*	3.5
23	1.6*	4.9*	2.2	0.3*	-4.8	-0.4*
24	8.3	12.1	11.2	5.7	1.0*	2.3
25	2.8*	1.6*	1.2*	0.1*	-4.5*	0.7*
26	4.8	5.7*	15.6	4.9	1.7*	12.2
27	-0.3*	-1.6*	NA	0.9	-2.8	0.7*
28	1.7	3.7*	6.6	2.3	-3.0	2.0
29	4.1	5.7*	12.2	5.6	4.1	5.0
30	5.8	5.2	11.9	4.5	1.6*	4.3
31	4.8	19.6*	9.9	5.8	-0.8*	5.3
32	5.4	6.6	6.8	3.9	0.4*	0.4*
33	4.6	-0.7*	9.7	3.8	0.9	0.8*
34	3.8	1.4*	7.2	1.7	-2.5*	3.6
35-6	5.4	4.0*	7.5	2.8	-1.4*	1.8
37	6.2	2.4*	10.3	3.7	-1.3*	1.8
38	5.6	12.9*	12.1	0.6*	1.0*	6.6
40	7.4	3.3*	10.0	6.3	-0.4*	2.0
41	-8.4*	-15.4*	NA	-6.1	11.2*	3.0
42	-9.7*	5.6*	10.4	5.8	-1.6*	5.7
74	14.5	10.0*	10.6	15.8	0.4*	5.9
Total	5.0	5.0	9.4	3.6	-2.3	2.7
CG	4.3	3.0*	7.8	3.1	-1.3*	3.8
IG	4.1	5.4	9.2	3.4	-0.6*	2.1
CNDG	4.0	5.3*	8.5	3.6	-4.1	2.7
CDG	5.1	8.8	11.4	2.6	0.4*	3.4
Sub-total	4.2	5.2	9.0	3.4	-2.4	2.7

NOTES: I Period from 1973-4 to 1982-3.
II Period from 1982-3 to 1986-7.
III Period from 1986-7 to 1997-8.
Growth rates are calculated by semi-log trends.
* Statistically insignificant at 95 per cent confidence level.
CG is capital goods; IG is intermediate goods
CNDG is consumer non-durable goods; CDG is consumer durable goods
Total includes NIC 20 to 74; Sub-total includes CG, IG, CNDG and CDG

SOURCE: Govt. of India, *Annual Survey of Industries: Summary Result of Factory Sector* (various issues).

A.K. Ghose ascribes the reason of the sharp decline of employment elasticity in the manufacturing organized sector during the 1980s to a strategy of capital deepening pursued by firms. The rise of the relative price of product wages encouraged modernization and pure substitution of capital for labour.[6] We examine the relationship between capital-labour ratio and product wages. In ASI the concept of workers includes all persons employed directly or through any agency and engaged in any manufacturing process or in cleaning any part of the machinery or premises used for manufacturing process or in any other kind of work incidental to the manufacturing process. Man-days are obtained by summing-up the number of workers attending in each shift over all the shifts worked on all days. Number of workers represents average daily employment. The figures are furnished by each factory by dividing the total man-days worked during a year by the total number of working days during the year. Thus, they are based on actual attendance and not on the physical number of persons on roll. Wages includes (a) direct wages and salary, i.e. basic wages and salaries, payment of overtime, dearness, compensatory, house rent and other allowance, (b) remuneration for period not worked, i.e. basic wages, salaries and allowance payable for leave period, paid holiday and lay-off payments, (c) bonuses and ex-gratia payment paid both at regular and less frequent intervals, i.e. incentive bonuses, good attendance bonuses, productive bonuses, profit sharing bonuses, etc.

When we analyse wage rates, we must take following three points into consideration. First, if workers work for more days during one year and man-days are same, number of workers will decrease. In fact, average annual working days of total industries rose from 273 days during the first period (1974-5 to 1982-3), to 300 days during the second period (1982-3 to 1986-7), to 309 days during the third period (1986-7 to 1996-7). Second, if workers attend to their work for longer than eight hours and get payments for overtime, man-days and number of workers may not come up although wages may rise. Third, if firms introduce contract or casual workers without replacing formal workers, man-days and number of workers may rise but wages grew less than them. Casual workers are getting lower salary than regular workers.

To calculate capital-labour ratio, we must estimate capital stock first. Capital stock is estimated by the perpetual inventory method. A capital stock in year T, denoted by K_T, is based on following formula:

$$K_T = K_0 + \sum_{t=1}^{T}(I_t - DS_t)$$

where K_0 is fixed capital stock in the benchmark year, I_t is the gross investment at constant price in fixed assets in year t, and DS_t is the amount of fixed assets at constant price discarded during year t. Hashim and Dadi estimate replacement value of fixed assets in 1960 after analysing the balance sheets of firms.[7] This study uses their estimate as benchmark. I_t is defined as

$$I_t = (B_t - B_{t-1} + D_t) / P_t$$

where B_t is the book value of fixed assets at the end of year t, D_t is the amount of depreciation allowances made during year t and P_t is the capital goods price deflator. It is difficult, however, to obtain data of DS_t. In this study we assume DS_t is zero.

To calculate product wages, wages to workers are deflated by the relevant wholesale price index of industries. Table 2 shows increase of product wages per man-day during the first period was insignificant at 95 per cent confidence level in many industries. But they grew rapidly during the second period. On the other hand, capital-labour ratio also came up during the second period. We can estimate two processes from the phenomenon. First, rapid increase of product wages might have encouraged modernization and pure substitution of capital for labour. As a result, capital-labour ratio jumped up. Second, investment increased to meet growing demand. After investment increased capital-labour ratio and labour productivity, wages rose.

We examine why product wages per man-day increased. Growth rates of labour costs during the second period were between 3.9 and 4.9 per cent at four used-basis industry groups. These figures are exaggerated by two reasons. First, product wages depend on the relative price of food. As workers spend a large proportion of wages to purchase food, all India consumer price index for industrial workers puts 57 per cent weight on food articles. The terms of trade between agriculture and manufacturing affect product wages.[8] During the second period, wholesale index of food items and consumer price index (CPI) for industrial workers grew by 7.4 and 8.0 per cent. They were higher than 5.7 per cent of wholesale index of manufacturing goods. Growth rates of real wage rates, which were deflated by CPI for industrial workers, were less than 3.1 per cent (Table 3). Second, product wages declined at four used-based industry groups after 1978-9 (Figure 1). As product wages were low in 1982-3, their growth

TABLE 2. GROWTH RATES OF PRODUCT WAGES AND LABOUR PRODUCTIVTY AND CAPITAL-LABOUR RATIO

(%)

NIC	*Product wages per man-day at 1981-2 prices*			*Labour productivity (GVA per man-day)*			*Capital-labour ratio (fixed capital per number of workers)*		
	I	*II*	*III*	*I*	*II*	*III*	*I*	*II*	*III*
20-1	2.4*	2.7	2.7	-0.0*	4.3*	4.8	3.2	12.8	5.8
22	-1.1*	5.9*	-0.7*	-13.4	9.5*	2.7	-1.2*	17.4	7.3
23	1.4*	6.6	-1.9	1.3*	8.0	2.7	5.7	10.2	7.8
24	2.9	7.9	3.7	0.9*	10.0	9.0	6.2	7.6	9.9
25	5.7	7.5*	-1.6*	3.6	4.5*	-0.7*	3.1	7.5*	3.1
26	5.2*	2.0*	0.4*	-1.3*	3.6*	4.9	11.3	8.4	4.4
27	-2.0	2.9*	-3.8*	-2.8	1.4*	0.3*	8.0	7.6*	7.3
28	1.4*	1.2	1.6	-2.2	5.6*	5.2	6.8	9.9	6.1
29	-3.5*	1.9*	1.6*	-4.3	0.8*	7.1	11.4	4.2	7.0
30	1.3*	6.9	1.5	-0.9*	3.1*	8.4	5.1	5.8	5.6
31	-3.8	6.5	3.9	-4.2	19.6	5.7	8.1	11.3	5.5
32	-1.0*	5.2	1.8	0.9*	5.5	5.7	4.3	13.3	9.1
33	-1.2*	0.1*	2.2	-1.0*	-2.4*	7.9	4.1	4.3	7.8
34	1.6	4.8	0.2	1.0*	2.8*	3.1	6.7	8.7	7.3
35-6	0.3*	4.3	1.9	0.2	4.3*	5.7	5.9	9.2	6.9
37	-1.2*	4.2	3.2	-0.1*	2.8*	8.9	9.4	8.6	5.9
38	-0.1*	6.3	0.4*	1.9*	11.2*	5.7	7.4	7.6	4.7
40	-1.4*	6.6	6.4*	-1.1*	3.8*	8.6	NA	NA	NA
41	-1.7*	4.9	1.7*	-0.4*	-26.2*	NA	NA	NA	NA
42	-3.6	5.5	3.5	-10.0	7.0*	5.4	NA	NA	NA
74	-2.6*	6.7	1.8	-5.6*	6.6*	5.7	NA	NA	NA
Total	0.4*	4.9	2.4	0.3*	5.3	6.9	5.5	9.7	6.4
CG	-1.7*	4.6	1.9	-1.9*	3.8*	4.0	6.7	7.4	3.4
IG	-0.4*	3.9	1.7	-0.2*	4.7*	7.2	5.7	8.0	7.3
CNDG	-0.0*	4.7	1.0	-0.2*	6.4	5.9	4.2	10.8	6.6
CDG	-0.1*	4.9*	3.1	0.3*	6.3*	8.0	6.0	9.2	6.6
Sub-total	-0.3*	4.5	1.7	-0.3*	5.5	6.3	5.4	9.6	6.4

NOTES: I Period from 1973-4 to 1982-3. In the case of Product wages and Labour productivity, from 1974-5 to 1982-3.

II Period from 1982-3 to 1986-7.

III Period from 1986-7 to 1997-8. In the case of Product wages and Labour productivity, from 1986-7 to 1996-7.

Growth rates are calculated by semi-log trends.

* Statistically insignificant at 95 per cent confidence level.

NA: Not available

SOURCE: As in Table 1.

TABLE 3. GROWTH RATES OF PRODUCT WAGE

(%)

Industry group	*Product wages per man-day at 1981-2 prices*				*Real wages per man-day at 1981-2 prices*		
	I	*II*	*1978-9 to 1986-7*	*III*	*I*	*II*	*III*
CG	-1.7*	4.6	1.5	1.9	1.8*	3.1	1.5
IG	-0.4*	3.9	2.7	1.7	2.4	3.1	1.6
CNDG	-0.0*	4.7	0.7	1.0	0.8*	2.1*	0.4*
CDG	-0.0*	4.9*	3.3	3.1	1.9	1.9*	1.2
Sub-total	-0.3*	4.5	1.6	1.7	1.7	2.7	1.1

NOTES: I Period from 1974-5 to 1982-3. Growth rates are calculated by semi-log trends.
II Period from 1982-3 to 1986-7. Growth rates are calculated by semi-log trends.
1978-9 to 1986-7 Growth rate are calculated by compound growth rates.
III Period from 1986-7 to 1996-7. Growth rates are calculated by semi-log trends.
* Statistically insignificant at 95 per cent confidence level.

SOURCE: As in Table 1.

rates during the second period were exaggerated. Absolute level of product wages of four used-based industry groups exceeded the level of 1978-9 after 1983-4. For entrepreneurs absolute level of wages is more important than their growth rates. If we calculate compound growth rates of product wages between 1978-9 and 1986-7, they are less than growth rates of the third period except intermediate and consumer durable goods. Product wages per man-day did not increase rapidly between 1978-9 and 1986-7.

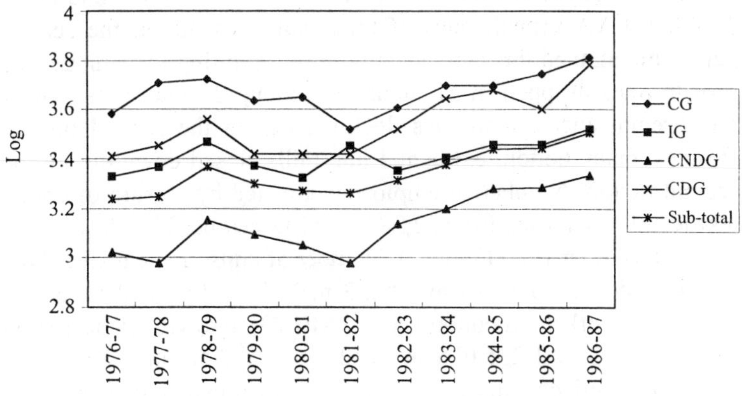

FIGURE 1. PRODUCT WAGES PER MAN-DAY

If product wages have nothing to do with capital-labour ratio, why growth rates of capital-labour ratio accelerated during the second period? If firms introduced new machinery for modernization or substitution for labour, it should have been reflected in production of capital goods and imports of capital goods. However, growth rates of GVA of capital goods industries and machinery and equipment other than transport equipment (NIC 35-6) went down from 4.3 per cent and 5.4 per cent during the first period to 3.0 per cent and 4.0 per cent during the second period. Imports of capital goods at 1981-2 price rose by 10.8 per cent because of import liberalization. Import share of domestic consumption of capital goods was still low because imports were regulated by quantitative control in spite of its relaxation. Total amount of output value and import of machinery and equipment other than transport equipment grew by 6.2 per cent during the second period. It was less than 6.9 per cent during the first period.

Table 4 shows growth rates of man-days, average working days and capital-man-days ratio. Since number of workers is derived as the ratio of man-days to working days, if working days rise more rapidly than man-days, number of workers decrease. In fact, average working days for one year rose during the second period.[9] That caused exaggevation of decrease of worker number during the second period. Therefore, capital-man-days ratio is better measure than capital-labour (number of workers) ratio.

There are two reasons of increase of capital-man-days ratio during the second period. First, negative growth of man-days pushed up capital-man-days ratio. India had recession between 1978-9 and 1982-3. While GVA growth rates of total industries during the second period maintained the same level with those during the first period, growth rates dropped in 11 industries among 21 industries. Under the circumstances, man-days declined during the second period. Besides, many cotton textile and jute mills closed down during the second period. Number of employees affected by closure of cotton textile mills increased from 32,387 on 31 December 1982 to 107,952 on 31 December 1986 (Table 5). Number of units in jute textile (NIC 25) went down from 219 in 1982-3 to 184 in 1986-7. As a result, number of workers in cotton textile (NIC 23) and NIC 25 decreased from 926,193 and 235,076 in 1982-3 to 788,740 and 191,436 in 1986-7 respectively. Many workers lost jobs without getting any compensation, which was guaranteed by law. The phenomena reduced

TABLE 4. GROWTH RATES OF MAN-DAYS, AVERAGE WORKING DAYS AND CAPITAL MAN-DAYS

(%)

NIC	*Man-days*			*Working days***			*Capital-man-days*		
	I	*II*	*III*	*I*	*II*	*III*	*I*	*II*	*III*
20-1	4.2	0.3*	3.1	177	235	264	4.0	6.5	5.4
22	13.7	-1.5*	4.1	222	263	288	-6.1	13.2	6.5
23	0.7*	-3.0*	-0.5*	285	311	318	5.3	8.5	7.6
24	7.3	2.1*	2.4	304	322	330	4.5	6.5	9.9
25	-0.1*	-2.9*	0.7*	308	304	311	4.2	5.9*	3.3
26	5.6	2.1*	12.7	279	292	298	7.9	8.1	3.9
27	2.5	-3.0	0.6*	273	285	288	6.0	7.7	7.5
28	3.9	-1.9*	2.1	303	313	318	5.2	8.7	6.0
29	8.0	4.9	5.7	275	294	295	8.3	3.4*	6.9
30	7.2	2.0	4.3	295	320	323	2.1*	5.4	5.5
31	7.9	-0.0*	5.6	285	312	317	5.3	10.6	5.4
32	5.1	1.1*	1.4	272	269	281	3.4	12.6	8.2
33	5.4	1.8*	1.0*	313	328	334	2.5*	3.4*	8.0
34	3.5	-1.4*	4.0	285	301	301	4.7	7.7	6.8
35-6	5.3	-0.3*	2.1	289	310	306	2.8	8.2	6.7
37	7.1	-0.4*	1.7	289	309	310	6.5	7.7	5.9
38	3.6	1.7*	6.5	282	298	298	4.8	7.0	4.8
40	10.2	-0.6*	1.6*	347	364	363	NA	NA	NA
41	-7.2	10.7*	2.9*	329	336	330	NA	NA	NA
42	8.8	-1.4*	6.7	349	359	362	NA	NA	NA
74	20.3	3.4*	6.5	255	306	319	NA	NA	NA
Total	5.0	-0.4*	2.8	273	300	309	4.3	7.5	6.3
CG	6.2	-0.9*	4.1	288	307	309	3.4	6.9	3.1
IG	4.5	0.8	2.3	283	300	309	4.5	6.7	7.2
CNDG	4.0	-1.0*	2.9	250	284	298	3.6	7.8	6.3
CDG	5.1	2.5*	3.5	282	311	307	3.3	7.0	6.6
Sub-total	4.5	-0.2*	2.9	266	294	303	4.1	7.4	6.3

NOTES: I Period from 1974-5 to 1982-3.
II Period from 1982-3 to 1986-7.
III Period from 1986-7 to 1996-7.
Growth rates were calculated by semi-log trends.
* Statistically insignificant at 95 per cent confidence level.
** Working days are calculated by dividing man-days by number of workers. As number of workers is furnished by each factory, these figures do not express exact ones. However, they suggest the trends.

SOURCE: As in Table 1.

incentive of worker to join labour unions. Memberships of workers' unions including service sector decreased from 8.18 million in 1986-7 to 5.61 million in 1996-7.[10] Closure of many mills gave big damage to labour union movement because labour union failed to protect job security. Figure 2 expresses that man-days lost by labour disputes dropped sharply during the second period. Moreover, man-days lost by lockout exceeded those by strike. It implies that bargaining power of labour unions declined. The second period was turning point of labour movement.

Second, the manufacturing sector had redundant workers in the late 1970s. Although growth rates of GVA declined, man-days increased during the recession period between 1978-9 and 1982-3. We estimate utilization rates of capacity on the basis of minimum capital-output ratio. Capital-output ratios are calculated. A benchmark year is then selected on the basis of the observed lowest capital-output ratio. The lowest observed capacity-output ratio is considered as capacity output. The estimate of capacity is obtained by dividing

TABLE 5. CLOSURE OF COTTON TEXTILE MILLS

	Number of mills	*Employees on roll*
31 December 1980	17	26,517
31 December 1981	37	78,397
31 December 1982	28	32,387
31 December 1983	63	94,431
31 December 1984	77	99,591
31 December 1985	78	107,221
31 December 1986	84	107,952

SOURCE: Govt. of India, *Annual Report of Ministry of Textile 1986-87*, p. 18.

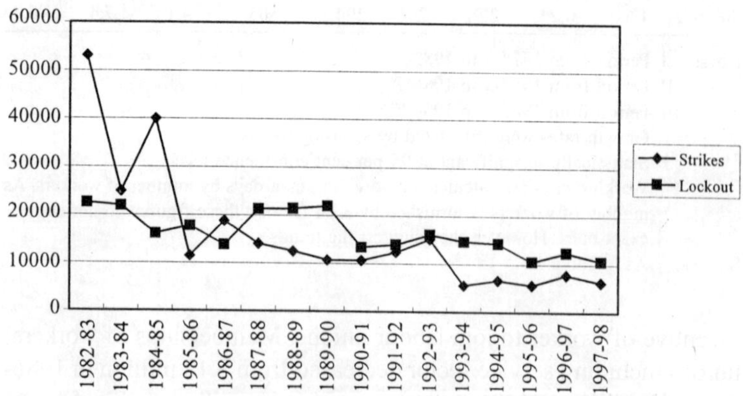

FIGURE 2. MAN-DAYS LOST BY DISPUTES

real fixed capital stock by minimum capital-output ratio. The utilization rate is given by actual output as a proportion of the estimated capacity.

Thus,

$$U = \frac{O}{\underline{C}} \cdot 100$$

$$\underline{C} = \frac{C}{(C/O)\ \text{min}}$$

where U is capacity utilization, O is GVA, $\underline{C}$ is estimate of capacity, C is capital stock. Capacity utilization rates dropped clearly at all industry groups after 1978-9 (Table 6). Under the underutilization of capacity, workers became redundant. It seems that strong labour union movement prevented large-scale retrenchment of workers up to 1982-3. Although product wages went down between 1978-9 and 1982-3, real wages did not decrease. Real wages per man-day in sub-total of four used-based industry groups at 1981-2 prices was Rs. 27 in both 1978-9 and 1982-3. From viewpoints of worker, real wages are more important than product wages.

During the third period, most of industries showed high growth of GVA. Under the background of slow rupee depreciation, export oriented industries like textile products (NIC 26) and leather products (NIC 29) developed. Besides, chemical products (NIC 30) and transport equipment grew. Investment and man-days increased to meet growing demand. Growth rates of man-days recovered during the third period although they were less than the first period. Employment elasticity during the third period was much less than that during the

TABLE 6. CAPACITY UTILIZATION RATES

(%)

	1977-8	*1978-9*	*1979-80*	*1980-1*	*1981-2*	*1982-3*	*1983-4*
CG	96.54	84.86	80.14	79.79	66.54	71.44	67.19
IG	98.03	100.00	87.52	78.32	78.68	79.9	76.19
CNDG	94.78	100.00	89.33	77.3	77.45	78.3	88.88
CDG	100.00	96.83	85.87	79.05	81.23	90.53	90.89
Sub-total	99.15	100.00	89.11	80.39	77.54	80.24	81.33

SOURCE: As in Table 1.

TABLE 7. EMPLOYMENT ELASTICITY AND SHARE OF WAGES IN GVA

NIC	*Employment elasticity*		*Share of product wage in GVA (%)*			
	I	*III*	*1973-4*	*1982-3*	*1986-7*	*1997-8*
20-1	0.490	0.311	24.8	25.3	22.4	17.8
22	0.827	0.486	25.2	37.8	26.7	18.9
23	0.179*	-0.010*	41.2	56.5	52.7	34.0
24	0.658	0.182	25.2	28.7	27.2	16.6
25	0.168*	0.272*	68.3	80.9	84.2	75.5
26	0.782	0.724	32.3	26.7	24.8	21.1
27	0.009*	-0.079*	34.1	33.1	32.1	26.4
28	0.902	0.279	31.3	35.1	28.5	25.9
29	1.002	0.391	44.4	36.8	37.6	20.8
30	0.666	0.354	14.9	14.6	16.4	10.4
31	0.647	0.493	19.5	14.2	10.8	12.7
32	0.615	0.076	33.8	23.1	23.8	14.8
33	0.717	0.095	29.5	26.7	30.8	12.9
34	0.447	0.437	29.6	27.8	30.0	21.8
35-6	0.482	0.241	24.7	22.7	22.7	16.3
37	0.594	0.196	40.0	32.6	33.6	22.8
38	0.082*	0.501	36.4	25.9	24.7	18.1
40	0.688	0.217	18.5	20.5	19.8	13.0
41	0.222*	0.085	23.0	10.2	36.7	2.4
42	-0.094*	0.532	6.2	47.4	42.8	41.4
74	1.044	0.514	21.5	21.1	22.7	21.4
Total	0.654	0.286	27.4	26.4	25.7	16.5
CG	0.594	0.462	30.1	26.8	27.7	24.8
IG	0.765	0.231	26.5	22.9	23.0	14.6
CNDG	0.755	0.308	32.4	34.0	31.1	18.8
CDG	0.447	0.299	31.4	25.0	23.7	15.6
Sub-total	0.740	0.302	29.6	27.6	26.7	17.7

NOTES: I Period from 1973-4 to 1982-3
III Period from 1986-7 to 1997-8
Employment elasticity is calculated by $\log E = \alpha + \beta \log G$. E is number of workers and G is GVA.
* Statistically insignificant at 90 per cent confidence level.

SOURCE: As in Table 1.

first period (Table 7). It decreased even in labour intensive industries like NIC 26 and 29. Economic liberalization forced domestic companies to introduce more capital-intensive technology to meet needs from market. Foreign collaboration companies demand domestic subcontracting companies to supply high quality parts. Domestic companies must improve their product quality to compete with imported products. Export-oriented unit is required to meet international standard quality. High quality control can save west of material costs. Investment became necessary to improve quality control even when cheap labour force was available. More capital-intensive technology was selected during the third period not to save labour costs but to improve quality control and save material costs. After companies introduced capital-intensive technology and improved labour productivity by rationalization, they retrenched redundant workers. Even benefit making companies introduced voluntary retirement scheme to implements rationalization.[11] As a result, the share of product wages in GVA dropped sharply during the third period. Growth rates of real product wages were not high in spite of rapid labour productivity increase during the third period. Growth rate of real product wages in total industries was 2.4 per cent. Growth of wages was not reason of increase of capital-labour ratio.

2. IMPACTS OF ECONOMIC REFORMS

To examine impact of economic reforms since 1991, the third period is divided into two sub-periods. Economic reforms brought investment boom between 1991-2 and 1995-6. As industrial licensing was abolished, firms could set up or expand their capacity by their own judgement. High growth rates of GVA generated the expectation that demand would increase further in the future. To meet growth of demands, gross fixed capital formation rose in the first half of 1990s. Moreover, stock boom and increase of internal financing encouraged the atmosphere. The three factors made entrepreneurs to overestimate growth rates of demand. GVA started declining or stagnating in the mid-1990s. As a result, underutilization of capacity made its appearance across the four industry groups.[12] Although capacity utilization rates of the four industry groups peaked in the mid-1990s, they witnessed a clear drop after the mid-1990s. Labour and capital productivity declined after the mid-1990s due to under-utilization.

Table 8 shows number of workers depends on growth rates of GVA. New units set up and existing units increased their employment and shifts to meet rising demand after economic reforms. As growth rates of GVA declined after 1995-6, many units closed down and number of workers also went down due to retrenchment of workers and reduction of shifts. Growth rates of worker numbers between 1991-2 and 1997-8 were higher than 5 per cent in NIC 26, 30, 31, 38, and 74, whose growth rates of GVA were higher than 8 per cent.

TABLE 8. GROWTH RATES OF GVA AND WORKER NUMBERS

(%)

NIC	*GVA at 1981-2 prices*			*Number of workers*		
	1986-7 to 1990-1	*1991-2 to 1995-6*	*1991-2 to 1997-8*	*1986-7 to 1990-1*	*1991-2 to 1995-6*	*1991-2 to 1997-8*
20-1	9.9	12.2	10.0	3.1	3.2	2.8
22	4.6	5.8*	7.3	6.2*	1.2*	2.3*
23	6.1*	2.6*	4.0*	-1.3*	1.4*	1.3*
24	15.2	15.1*	10.1*	0.9*	5.5	3.9
25	-6.5	2.2*	4.1*	-0.1*	4.6*	2.7*
26	20.8	16.3*	8.3*	12.3	17.7	12.9
27	12.0	-7.3*	-0.4*	-1.3*	3.8	2.9
28	8.5	13.5	7.5*	0.1*	4.0	2.5
29	15.5	8.8*	7.0*	10.5	5.8	2.9*
30	14.8	15.3	11.0	3.6	5.5	5.1
31	10.3	15.2	9.2*	5.9	6.0	5.5
32	13.1	4.1*	4.1*	0.7	0.4*	-0.3*
33	11.6	17.6	15.0	-1.2*	3.8*	1.8*
34	3.4*	15.3	11.5	5.7	4.4*	4.7
35-6	9.2	11.0	8.2	2.2*	3.2*	1.9*
37	7.8	18.9	15.4	-0.8*	5.4	3.3*
38	3.2*	17.0*	12.6	5.6	9.6	8.0
40	9.3	15.5	10.4	1.2*	8.7	4.5*
41	NA	59.3*	43.6*	0.7*	-3.0*	-1.0*
42	10.4*	17.1	8.5*	5.1*	10.3	4.6*
74	13.2	13.6*	10.7*	7.5*	9.4	6.8
Total	10.6	13.6	10.2	2.5	4.4	3.4
CG	8.3	11.8	9.7	5.1	3.7*	3.1
IG	12.6	14.7	10.5	1.2	4.1*	3.1
CNDG	10.2	10.9	9.2	2.7	3.8	3.1
CDG	10.1	14.9	13.5	3.5	5.3	5.0
Sub-total	10.8	13.0	10.3	2.7	4.0	3.2

NOTES: Growth rates are calculated by semi-log trends.
* Statistically insignificant at 95 per cent confidence level.

SOURCE: As in Table 1.

To examine which sector absorbed employment, we calculate compound growth rates of worker numbers (Table 9). The organized sector, i.e. the factory sector consists of the census and sample sectors. It covers all factories registered under the Factory Act which refer to the establishments using power and employing 10 or more workers and those not using power and employing 20 or more workers. The census sector includes all units employing 100 or more workers irrespective of the use of power. The sample sector covers the rest in the organized sector.

TABLE 9. COMPOUND GROWTH RATES OF WORKER NUMBER AND UNIT NUMBER

(%)

Sector	*1990-1 to 1995-6*			*1990-1 to 1996-7*		
	Public	*Private*	*Total*	*Public*	*Private*	*Total*
Number of Workers						
Sample	-11.3	3.5	2.5	-8.5	4.3	3.5
Census	-0.2	4.3	2.6	-4.7	2.5	0.0
Number of Units						
Sample	-12.8	3.8	3.0	-8.7	3.4	2.8
Census	-0.6	0.4	0.2	-3.3	0.2	-0.5

SOURCE: Govt. of India, *Annual Survey of Industries: Summary Report on Absenteeism, Labour Turnover, Employment and Labour Cost* (various issues).

The sample sector has advantage at four points: (1) cheap labour costs, (2) no job security regulation, (3) low overhead costs, and (4) easy adjustment to change of market. On the other hand, the census sector has advantage at two points: (1) economies of scale and (2) strong financial base. In 1990-1 average labour costs per man-day worked were Rs. 122.0, Rs. 99.1, Rs. 75.3 and Rs. 51.5 in census public, census private, sample public and sample private units respectively. Employments went down in the sample public sector between 1990-1 and 1995-6. As the public sector accounted for only 9.1 per cent of worker numbers of the sample sector in 1990-1, the effect was negligible. In the census public sector, number of workers and units went down by 0.2 per cent and 0.6 per cent respectively. Although units increased slightly in the census private sector, number of workers came up by 4.3 per cent. Many new units set up in the sample private sector in the 1990s. Number of units and workers grew by 3.8 per cent and 3.5 per cent respectively.

We can conclude two points from the above analysis. First, the pubic sector reduced employments in the 1990s. While the public sector decreased employments, the private sector increased them. It does not mean, however, that private units have financial stability. 3,296 cases were registered as sick companies at Board for Industrial and Financial Reconstruction on 31 December 2000. The criteria to determine sickness in an industrial company are that (1) the accumulated losses of the company to be equal to or more than its net worth, i.e. its paid-up capital plus its free reserves, (2) the company should have completed five years after incorporation under the

Companies Act, 1956, (3) it should have 50 or more workers on any day of the 12 months preceding the end of the financial year with reference to which sickness is claimed. Among 3,296 cases, 3,121 are private units, 74 are central public sector units, 101 are state public sector units.[13] Although many private units closed down in the 1990s, many units set up. As a result, number of units rose. Second, there is no clear difference between the census and sample private sectors. Between 1990-1 and 1995-6 the census private sector gained more employments than the sample private sector. As the census private sector lost employment in 1996-7, growth rate of worker number was 2.5 per cent between 1990-1 and 1996-7. On the other

TABLE 10. COMPOUND GROWTH RATES OF REAL LABOUR COSTS* PER MAN-DAY BETWEEN 1990-1 AND 1996-7

(%)

NIC	*Sample*		*Census*	
	Public	*Private*	*Public*	*Private*
20	4.2	2.1	2.6	2.3
21	9.3	3.3	3.2	0.0
22	2.5	10.5	-17.0	-1.0
23	4.1	0.7	-0.2	-1.5
24	-13.2	0.3	-1.0	0.1
25	8.0	-1.7	-1.6	-0.7
26	8.9	-0.3	-5.1	0.0
27	1.1	1.7	5.0	-0.9
28	5.5	2.3	2.4	5.0
29	8.7	0.5	-2.2	-2.4
30	6.0	2.7	2.6	0.4
31	6.3	1.7	4.2	1.5
32	7.2	2.0	5.3	1.6
33	-2.1	0.2	4.6	0.4
34	29.8	0.8	4.6	1.4
35	6.0	3.6	4.4	2.5
36	14.5	-0.1	3.6	1.1
37	8.1	3.1	5.2	1.1
38	-9.2	2.2	1.6	4.4
39	1.7	3.6	1.4	2.0
41	NA	NA	6.2	8.1
42	3.4	-4.8	1.3	0.6
74	0.8	0.5	11.9	1.2
97	-2.8	2.2	3.2	3.7
All	6.0	3.5	3.2	1.0

NOTE: * At 1980-1 prices.
SOURCE: As in Table 9.

hand, the sample private sector increased employment by 4.3 per cent during the same period.

ILO report argues that government interventions played a key role in determining wages in the organized sector. The interventions include setting of minimum wage norms, direct determination of wages in public enterprises, indirect influence on wage determination in private enterprises through the establishment of Wage Boards, setting of norms for wage differentials and establishment of rules of indexation and bonus payment.[14] If the argument is right, labour costs of the census private sector might have correlation with those of the census public sector. Labour costs include salary and wages, bonus, provident and other fund, and workmen and staff expenses. Table 10 shows that growth rates of labour costs in both sectors did not have correlation. Simple correlation coefficient of 24 industries is 0.395. Besides, it is noteworthy that labour costs per man-day of sample private sector increased faster than that of census private sector in 12 industries among 23 industries although their gap was still large. The census private sector might have been affected more than the sample private sector by the influence of the government intervention due to pressure of labour unions. It seems that reasons other than the government intervention push up labour costs in the sample private sector.

3. THE RISE OF MEDIUM-SIZE UNITS

B. Goldar points out long-term shift of employments from units employing 2,000 and above to units employing 50 to 499 during the 1980s and 1990s.[15] Table 11 shows distribution of employments by employment size. The share of units employing 1,000 and above declined clearly. Closure of many large-scale cotton and jute mills might have been a reason. On the other hand, the share of medium scale units employing 50 to 199 rose. Medium scale units gained employments. The classification of census and sample sectors is not appropriate to analyse medium-class units because they belong to both sectors.

We examine condition of medium-class units from a long-term viewpoint. If GVA is the sum of profits (P) and total emoluments for employees including white collar (E), and if N indicates number of employees, the labour productivity is given by (P+E)/N. If K_1 is

TABLE 11. DISTRIBUTION OF EMPLOYMENTS BY EMPLOYMENT SIZE

(%)

Employment size	*1973-4*	*1980-1*	*1990-1*	*1995-6*	*1997-8*
Less than 50	14.4	13.8	17.5	16.8	16.8
50-99	8.2	9.0	10.8	11.7	13.1
100-199	9.4	9.2	10.7	13.0	12.9
200-499	13.1	12.1	13.5	17.3	19.0
500-999	11.6	9.7	12.0	14.3	13.6
1,000 and above	43.3	46.3	35.5	26.9	24.6

SOURCE: As in Table 1.

productive capital, which consists of fixed capital and working capital and K_2 is fixed capital stock, the following identity is established:

$$\frac{P+E}{N}=\frac{P}{N}+\frac{E}{N}=\frac{K_2}{N}\;\frac{K_1}{K_2}\;\frac{P}{K_1}+\frac{E}{N}$$

The labour productivity may be broken down into profit per employee and labour cost per employee, and the former may be rewritten as the product of capital-labour ratio, the ratio of productive capital to fixed capital stock, and gross capital-profit ratio. Data is available after 1979-80 onwards. Table 12 shows employment size-wise labour productivity.

The three points are noteworthy. First, average gross profit ratio between 1979-80 and 1997-8 was highest in units employing 50 to 99, second in units employing 100 to 199 and lowest in units employing 1,000 and above. Medium scale units were dynamic sector to gain employment and investment. Although many medium-class units closed down due to financial weakness, more units set up to get higher profits in the 1980s and 1990s. That is a reason that medium-class units increased employments.[16] It does not mean, however, that medium-class units were more profitable than large units in the same industry. Units employing 1,000 and above included many units of cotton and jute textiles. Number of workers per unit in the census sector in 1990-1 was 625 in public sector of NIC 23, 1,851 in public sector of NIC 25 and 1,496 in private sector of NIC 25. Real growth rates of GVA were very low in these two industries during the third period. As many units in the two industries were making loss, average gross profit ratio was low. On the other hand, number of workers per unit in the census sector in 1990-1 was 101, 132 and 132 in private sector of NIC 26, 29, 30, whose growth rates of GVA were

TABLE 12. GROWTH RATES OF LABOUR PRODUCTIVITY

Employment Size	*(P+E)/N (Rs.)*	*K_2/N (Rs.)*	*P/K_1 (%)*	*E/N (Rs.)*
1979-80				
Less than 50	11,435	58,826	29.4	4,330
50-99	12,161	51,948	32.9	4,966
100-199	15,384	77,181	35.6	6,024
200-499	21,239	161,147	37.3	7,833
500-999	27,750	276,544	21.9	10,518
1,000 and above	24,434	252,901	13.9	11,483
1995-6				
Less than 50	26,297	120,968	19.9	7,973
50-99	32,709	88,287	35.8	8,286
100-199	51,081	156,303	30.7	12,482
200-499	57,562	249,534	25.5	15,543
500-999	71,875	354,776	26.2	18,624
1,000 and above	75,322	572,011	24.7	22,467
1997-8				
Less than 50	35,440	113,888	31.0	9,040
50-99	34,430	97,932	30.9	9,148
100-199	55,099	206,121	24.7	13,782
200-499	59,614	268,071	21.4	17,524
500-999	78,238	433,627	19.9	20,119
1,000 and above	81,400	642,360	22.8	23,587
Growth rates (%)				
Less than 50	6.0	3.4	30.7*	3.6
50-99	6.4	3.4	33.5*	3.4
100-199	7.4	4.7	31.3*	4.5
200-499	6.9	3.1	30.2*	4.3
500-999	6.2	2.2	24.2*	3.5
1,000 and above	7.2	5.4	18.0*	4.1

NOTES: Growth rates were calculated by semi-log trends.
* Average between 1979-80 and 1997-8.

SOURCE: As in Table 1.

higher than 10 per cent during the same period. As average number of workers per unit in total industries of the census sector was 165, unit size was below average in the three industries. Units of the three industries contributed to improvement of average gross profit ratio in medium scale units.

Number of workers per unit had shrunk during the 1970s. However, the trend stopped in the mid-1980s. Worker number per unit of total industries (NIC 20-1 to 38) in the organized sector was 69 in 1973-4. It decreased to 53 in 1985-6 and changed between 50 and 54 after 1985-6 onwards. M. Alam and S.N. Mishra ascribe decline of average employment size per unit to the rigidities of labour legislation and a rise in the incidence of redundancy among a large number of city-based industrial units.[17] However, shrinkage of employment size could be observed in few industries. To examine which industry decreased worker number per unit, its growth rates are calculated, on the basis of semi-log trends. Among 17 industries (NIC 20-1 to 38), only NIC 20-1, 23, 25, 32 and 37 showed higher than1 per cent negative growth rates at 95 per cent confidence level and above between 1979-80 and 1997-8. On the other hand, NIC 22, 24, 26 and 38 showed higher than 1 per cent positive growth rates. It can be seen that disparities of gross profit ratio did not arise as a result of differences of employment size within the same industry. The profit differential among industries might be reflected in different gross profit ratio of employment size.

Second, the labour productivity differential had been large. Small-scale units had weakness in that sense. While many large size units employing 1,000 and above closed down, remaining large units invested in equipment to improve productivity.

Third, labour costs per employee rose fastest in units employing 100 to 199. Faster rise of product wages did not prevent increase of employments in the units. The share of units employing 100 to 199 in total employees of the factory sector rose from 9.2 per cent in 1980-1 to 12.9 per cent in 1997-8.

P.R. Fallon and R.E.B. Lucas observe that job security regulation affected growth of employments in the census sector after 1976. Industrial Disputes Act was amended in 1976. The amendment prohibited lay-off, retrenchment and closure by industrial units employing not less than 300 workers without prior permission of the government. In 1982 the coverage was extended to include industrial units employing 100 and more workers. ILO report also argues that employment seculity regulations induced employers to keep the establishments size artificially small, partially sacrificing economies of scale.[18] However, units employing 100 to 199 developed well along with units employing 50 to 99.

4. TRADE UNION AND INSTITUTION

It has been argued that strong labour union has made labour market rigid. Many sick cotton textile mills had been taken over by the government under the pretext of labour protection. After labour unions failed to prevent closure of many units, power of labour unions has declined since the mid-1980s. Decline of labour unions induced two phenomena.

First, employers started introduction of contract worker to make employment flexible and to save labour costs. Table 13 shows sector-wise percentage of man-days worked by contract workers. The figure does not include casual workers out of workshop. The percentage may be higher if these workers are included. In the census sector the share rose during the 1980s and 1990s. Although the percentage dropped sharply in some industries like NIC 22 and 29 in the sample sector, it increased in many industries in the sector. Employers were using contract worker as buffer of employment.

Second, employers retrenched workers by voluntary retirement scheme. However, redeployment of workers was constrained by lack of large-scale training facilities and poor adaptability among the older workers.[19] Many workers started working as casual labourers.[20] If the income gap between the organized and the unorganized sectors is taken into consideration, it is difficult to maintain the same life standard before retirement. Workers of closed units had the same problem. A survey of the economic activities of displaced workers was conducted by Gandhi Labour Institute in 1984. The closures of a large number of textile mills in Ahmedabad during two years of 1983-4 rendered about 36,000 workers jobless. Different workers supplied information about a period of one week in September 1984. Among 5,773 displaced workers, only 44 per cent reported to have had some earning activity in Ahmedabad during the reference week. In other words, more than half displaced workers did not have any earning activity.[21] After economic reforms, employment situation deteriorated further. Between March 1994 and the autumn of 1996,

TABLE 13. SECTOR-WISE PERCENTAGE OF MAN-DAYS WORKED BY CONTRACT WORKERS

(%)

	1980-1			*1990-1*			*1996-7*		
	Public	*Private*	*All*	*Public*	*Private*	*All*	*Public*	*Private*	*All*
Sample	NA	NA	NA	5.8	21.4	19.9	5.4	17.2	16.6
Census	1.9	6.1	4.6	5.3	10.9	9.1	7.3	17.3	14.2

SOURCE: As in Table 9.

52 out of 63 composite mills in Ahmedabad closed. The study of J. Howell and U. Kambhampati shows that conditions of retrenched workers did not improved from 1980s.[22]

In 1992 the government established the National Renewal Fund (NRF) to finance retraining and redeployment schemes and compensates the displaced workers. However, the scheme was not working effectively due to two reasons. First, funds were not enough to give compensation to redundant workers. Second, participation rates of training programmes were low because of a lack of confidence to obtain employment after training.[23] Sudden inflow of many retrenched workers into labour market induced over supply of labour force. Under the condition, workers could not have good prospect to find any earning activity in not only organized sector but also unorganized sector.

CONCLUSION

Manufacturing organized sector faced recession and utilization rates of capacity went down between 1978-9 and 1982-3. Although workers became redundant, strong labour union movement prevented large-scale retrenchment of workers and maintained real wage at the same level up to 1982-3. However, after many cotton textile and jute mills closed down during the mid-1980s, labour union movement declined. Closure of many mills gave big damage to labour union movement because labour union failed to protect job security.

In the 1980s economic growth without increase of employment became an issue. It was argued that rapid increase of wages encouraged modernization and pure substitution of capital for labour. Product wages rose rapidly because they decreased between 1978-9 and 1982-3. Absolute level of product wages in total four used-based industry groups exceeded the level of 1978-9 after 1983-4. Capital-man-days ratio jumped up between 1982-3 and 1986-7 due to two reasons. First, negative growth of man-days pushed up capital-man-days ratio. While GVA growth rates of total industries during the second period maintained the same level with those during the first period, they dropped in 11 industries among 21 industries. Under the circumstances, man-days declined during the second period. Besides, many cotton textile and jute mills closed down during the period. Second, the manufacturing sector had redundant workers in the late 1970s.

Growth rates of man-days recovered during the third period although they were less than the first period. Economic liberalization forced firms to introduce more capital-intensive technology and improve labour productivity to survive competition. After forms introduced capital-intensive technology and improve labour productivity by rationalization, they retrenched redundant workers. As a result, the share of product wages in GVA dropped sharply during the third period.

Medium-scale units employing 50 to 199 gained employment during the 1980s and 1990s. Average gross profit ratio between 1979-80 and 1997-8 was highest in units employing 50 to 99, second in units employing 100 to 199. In organised sector, worker number per unit did not changed in most of industries. It can be seen that disparities of gross profit ratio did not arise as a result of differences of employment size within the same industry. It has been argued that job security regulation affected growth of employments in the census sector after 1976. However, units employing 100 to 199 developed well along with units employing 50 to 99.

Although many workers were retrenched by closure of units and voluntary retirement scheme, redeployment of workers is constrained by lack of large-scale training facilities and poor adaptability among the older workers.

NOTES

1. P.R. Fallon and R.E.B. Lucas, 'Job Security Regulation and the Dynamic Demand for Industrial Labor in India and Zimbabwe', *Journal of Development Economics*, vol. 40, 1993.
2. I.J. Ahluwalia, *Productivity and Growth in Indian Manufacturing*, Delhi, Oxford University Press, 1992. A.K. Ghose, 'Employment in Organized Manufacturing in India', *The Indian Journal of Labour Economics*, April-June 1994.
3. B. Goldar Employment, 'Growth in Organised Manufacturing in India', *Economic and Political Weekly*, 1 April 2000.
4. Tirthankar Roy points out employment growth rates accelerated in consumer non-durable goods industry from the late 1980s. (Tirthankar Roy, 'Consumer Non-Durable Goods Industries: Growing Market and Increasing Competition', in Shuji Uchikawa (ed.), *Economic Reforms and Industrial Structure in India*, Delhi, Manohar, 2002, p. 92.)
5. This figure includes NIC 20 to 42 and 74. NIC 97 is excluded because its coverage shrunk after 1989-90 onwards.

6. A.K. Ghose, op. cit., p. 159.
7. The estimation by Hashim and Dadhi depends on old NIC (1960) code classification. We make arrangement to adjust to 1987 code (S.R. Hashim and M.M. Dadhi, *Capital-Output Relations in Indian Manufacturing*, M.S. University of Baroda, Baroda, 1973, p. 45). To connect 1960 code to 1987 code, four digit level data are required. Between 1959 and 1971-2 data of the sample sector is available only on three digit levels. Data of the sample sector are divided by the proportion of the census sector.

NIC 1987 code classification		*NIC 1960 code classification*	
20-1	Food products	20	Food products
22	Beverages and Tobacco	21	Beverages
23	Cotton textiles	22	Tobacco
24	Wool, silk and man-made fibre textiles	23	Textiles
25	Jute textiles	24	Footwear and wearing apparel
26	Textile products	25	Wood and cork products
27	Wood and wood products	26	Furniture and fixtures
28	Paper and paper products	27	Paper and paper products
29	Leather and fur products	28	Printing and publishing
30	Chemical and chemical products	29	Leather and fur produces
31	Rubber and plastic and petroleum products	31	Chemicals
		30	Rubber products
32	Non-metallic mineral products	32	Products of petroleum and coal
33	Basic mineral and alloys	33	Non-metallic mineral products
34	Metal products and parts	34	Iron and steel-basic metal
35-6	Machinery and equipment	35	Metal products
37	Transport equipment	36	Non-electrical machinery
38	Other manufacturing industries	37	Electrical machinery
39	Repair of capital goods	38	Transport equipment
40	Electricity generation, transmission and distribution	39	Other manufacturing industries
41	Gas and steam generation		
42	Water supply		
74	Storage and warehousing service		
97	Repair service		

8. A.K. Ghose, op. cit., pp. 156-7.
9. This point was emphasized by R. Nagaraj. (R. Nagaraj, 'Employment and Wages in Manufacturing Industries: Trends, Hypothesis and Evidence', *Economic and Political Weekly,* 22 Jan. 1994.)
10. Govt. of India, *Indian Labour Statistics* (various issues).
11. Some automobile and auto components manufacturers which author visited are implementing rationalization. They are making profits, introducing more advanced technology and retrenching workers by voluntary retirement scheme.

12. Shuji Uchikawa, 'Investment Boom and Capital Goods Industry', *Economic Reforms and Industrial Structure in India,* Delhi, Manohar, 2002, p. 40.
13. Homepage of Board of Industrial and Financial Construction (http://bifr.nic.in).
14. ILO, *India: Economic Reforms and Labour Policies*, New Delhi, 1996, p. 49.
15. B. Goldar, op. cit., p. 1193.
16. The same phenomena could be observed in Japan during the 1950s and 1960s. Small and medium size business is characterized by a high start-up, high failure rate. (Takafusa Nakamura, *The Postwar Japanese Economy: Its Development and Structure, 1974-1994*, Tokyo, University of Tokyo Press, 1995, p. 175.)
17. Moneer Alam and S.N. Mishra, 'Structural Reforms and Employment Issues in India: A Case of Industrial Labour', *The Indian Journal of Labour Economics*, vol. 41, no. 2, 1998, p. 284.
18. ILO, op. cit., p. 78.
19. Moneer Alam and S.N. Mishra, op. cit., p. 284.
20. R.C. Datta, 'New Technology and Textile Workers', *Economic and Political Weekly*, 25 Sep. 1999, p. L43.
21. B.B. Patel, *Workers of Closed Textile Mills*, Delhi, Oxford & IBH, 1988, p. 24.
22. Jude Howell and Uma Kambhampati, 'Liberalization and Labour: The Fate of Retrenched Workers in the Cotton Textile Industry in India', *Oxford Development Studies*, vol. 27, no. 1, 1999, p. 114.
23. Ibid., p. 117.

Economic Reforms and Labour Markets in India: Organized and Unorganized Sectors

JEEMOL UNNI

INTRODUCTION

The dominant view in today's world is that a flexible economy, one that can readily adjust to the needs of time, will achieve faster development than an economy with a rigid structure. An inflexible economy is more easily prone to bottlenecks due to mismatch of demand and supply leading to inflationary pressures and other economic dislocations. A flexible economy is one where individuals, firms, organizations and institutions efficiently adjust their goals and resources to changing constraints and opportunities (Killick 1995). This involves flexibility in all the markets, that is, land, capital, financial, labour and product markets. One well researched aspect of market efficiency bearing on adaptability or flexibility of the economy is the operation of labour markets. The notion of labour market flexibility has been given different meanings but revolve around the idea of the capacity to adapt to change.

This notion of flexibility was endorsed by the Washington Consensus with its focus on economic growth, mainly gross domestic product, and the improvement of resource allocation, through trade liberalization, privatization and stabilization. The emphasis on adjustment policies under this consensus had relegated the discussion on inequality to the sidelines, notwithstanding a greater concern for poverty in the 1990s. One view was that the best way to tackle poverty is to grow out of it. The other regarded measures to reduce inequality detrimental to growth and therefore not warranted during periods of adjustment when the emphasis was on reviving growth (van der Hoeven 2001).

In recent years Stiglitz, while holding the positions of the Senior Vice-President and Chief Economist of the World Bank, presented the view that the Washington Consensus had gone astray. It focused too much on price stability, rather than growth and the stability of output (Stiglitz 1998). There has been some rethinking on the broad objectives of the Washington Consensus. There is a broad consensus that the overall goal of development of a nation should be reduction of poverty, provision of employment and social inclusion of all parts of society. That is, labour market policies need to focus on the dynamic function of labour markets with greater investment in human capital, equity and social cohesion since these aspects contribute to higher growth and foster poverty alleviation.

India embarked on the structural adjustment programme in 1991, broadly following the dictates of the Washington Consensus. It is now a decade since the policies of liberalization, stabilization and privatization have been introduced, albeit slowly, in the Indian economy. What has this meant for economic growth and the labour markets in India? This paper will analyse the economic growth in the country prior to and after the reforms package was introduced and discuss its impact on the labour market.

GROWTH OF GDP BY SECTORS

India has enjoyed an annual growth rate of gross domestic product (GDP) of more than 6 per cent for nearly a decade. This is quite exceptional for any country. To take a slightly longer term view of the economy the annual growth rate of GDP and non-agricultural GDP have been plotted for the period 1975-6 to 1999-00 (Figure 1).

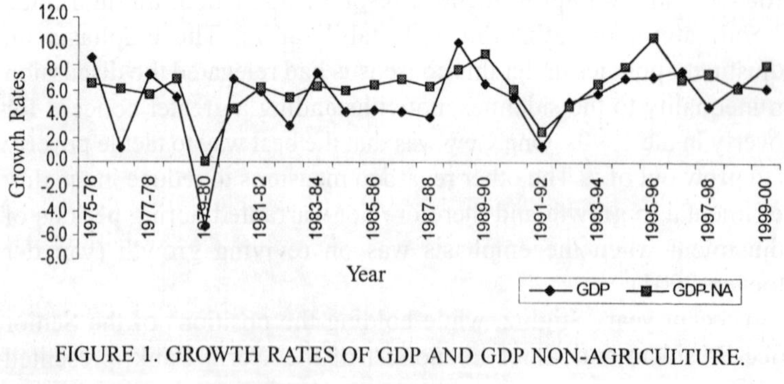

FIGURE 1. GROWTH RATES OF GDP AND GDP NON-AGRICULTURE.

TABLE 1. AVERAGE ANNUAL GROWTH RATES OF GDP, GDP IN NON-AGRICULTURE, PRIMARY, SECONDARY AND TERTIARY SECTOR

Years	*Annual Growth Rates of*				
	GDP	*GDP non-agriculture*	*Primary sector*	*Secondary sector*	*Tertiary sector*
1975-6	8.6	6.5	12.1	5.9	6.6
1976-7	1.2	6.0	-5.5	8.8	4.5
1977-8	7.2	5.6	9.3	7.0	4.8
1978-9	5.4	6.8	2.3	7.7	6.5
1979-80	-5.3	0.1	-13.0	-3.5	2.2
1980-1	6.9	4.5	12.1	3.9	4.4
1981-2	5.8	6.2	5.5	7.2	5.3
1982-3	3.0	5.4	0.0	2.8	6.5
1983-4	7.4	6.3	8.8	8.3	5.4
1984-5	4.2	5.9	1.5	6.0	6.1
1985-6	4.4	6.5	1.0	4.6	7.6
1986-7	4.2	6.9	0.2	6.0	7.1
1987-8	3.8	6.3	-1.0	6.7	6.3
1988-9	10.0	7.7	14.4	8.3	7.0
1989-90	6.5	9.0	1.9	10.1	8.5
1990-1	5.4	6.1	4.5	7.2	5.2
1991-2	1.3	2.6	-1.1	-1.0	4.7
1992-3	5.0	4.7	5.3	4.2	5.2
1993-4	5.7	6.5	3.8	5.5	7.4
1994-5	7.0	7.9	5.2	9.8	6.8
1995-6	7.1	10.4	-0.3	11.6	9.9
1996-7	7.5	6.9	8.5	7.5	7.0
1997-8	4.7	7.3	-1.5	3.7	9.3
1998-9	6.4	6.2	6.4	3.6	7.9
1999-00	6.2	8.1	0.8	6.7	9.2

SOURCES: 1. National Accounts Statistics Back Series 1950-1 to 1992-3; Central Statistical Organization, 2001.
2. National Account Statistics, 2001; Central Statistical Organization.

Large year to year fluctuations in the GDP growth is mainly due to the agricultural sector which is still to a large extent dependent on the vagaries of the monsoon. The trend of growth of GDP in non-agriculture is relatively smooth and can be categorized into five sub-periods over the long period since 1975-6. The period 1975-6 to 1980-1 was a period of slow growth though the economy was hit by the oil shock during this period (Table 1). The Government of India introduced a process of partial liberalization since 1980-1. The period 1980-1 to 1990-1 can be seen as a period of slow picking up of the economy (Morris, 1997). The structural adjustment programme and the economic reforms were introduced in June 1991. The first two years 1991-2 and 1992-3 were years of adjustment when the growth rates in non-agriculture dropped sharply. The period after these initial years of reform can again be divided into two. A period of rapid 'glorious' growth lasted from 1993-4 to 1996-7. Thereafter the economy has dropped into a period of recession till 1999-2000.

The non-agricultural sector is further divided into the secondary and tertiary sectors. The annual rate of growth of GDP of the primary, tertiary and secondary sectors is plotted in Figure 2. An interesting phenomenon is that the growth of GDP closely follows the growth of the primary sector, mainly agriculture, till 1992-3. Thereafter the link between the overall GDP growth and the agricultural sector is weak. This is due to the rapid growth of the non-agricultural sector after the introduction of economic reforms. Further, during the period of glorious growth, 1992-3 to 1996-7, both the secondary and tertiary sectors grew rapidly. However, during the period of recession while the growth of the secondary sector dropped, the tertiary sector continued a slow growth. This continued growth of the tertiary sector in the latter period is mainly what helped to weaken the link between the growth of agriculture and GDP.[1]

In this paper we analyse the patterns of growth in incomes and employment. A dynamic element was introduced in the economy in 1991 with the structural adjustment programme. The economic reforms were an attempt to introduce flexibility into the system. In

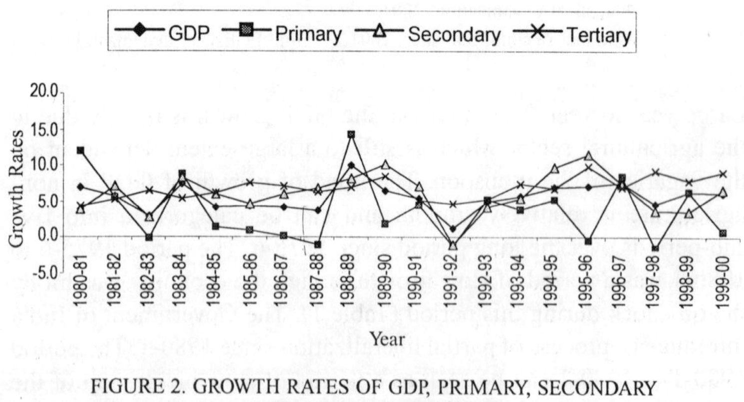

FIGURE 2. GROWTH RATES OF GDP, PRIMARY, SECONDARY AND TERTIARY SECTORS.

order to see the impact of reforms on the growth of employment we divide the entire period 1983 to 2000 into two sub-periods: broadly the pre-reforms period 1983 to 1993-4 and the reforms period, 1993-4 to 1999-00.[2] While the break in the period is mainly dictated by the availability of data on employment, it can also be justified on the ground that the economy began responding to the economic reforms in 1993-4, after the initial two years of adjustment. In that sense it is a good point from which to judge the impact of the reforms. Thc first period covers the pre-reforms and the beginning of rapid growth in the reforms period. The second period, however, covers both the period of rapid growth and the recession. The impact of the recession was felt in the year 1999-00 and hence the growth depicted by the second period already includes the slackening of growth after the first blush of successful impact of the reforms.

TABLE 2. GROWTH RATES OF GDP, EMPLOYMENT AND LABOUR PRODUCTIVITY, 1983-2000

Industrial Sector		*1983-94*	*1994-2000*	*1983-2000*
Total	NDP	5.7 (5.4)	6.4 (6.3) [3.6]	6.1 (6.2)
	Employment	2.0	1.0	1.6
	Labour Productivity	3.7	5.4	4.3
Agriculture	NDP	3.9 (3.3)	3.0 (3.1) [3.0]	3.6 (3.2)
	Employment	1.4	–0.1	0.8
	Labour Productivity	2.6	3.1	2.8
Non-agriculture	NDP	6.4 (6.5)	7.8 (7.7) [2.3]	6.9 (7.2)
	Employment	3.3	2.7	3.1
	Labour Productivity	3.1	5.1	3.8

NOTE:
1. These estimates are point-to-point estimates of exponential growth.
2. The figures in parenthesis are growth rates obtained by fitting a time trend.
3. Figures in square brackets are t-statistics for the significance of difference in the growth rates between the two periods using a dummy variable.

SOURCES:
1. National Accounts Statistics, Factor Incomes (New Series), 1980-1 to 1989-90; Central Statistical Organization, 1994.
2. National Account Statistics, 1996, 1997, 1998, 2001; Central Statistical Organization.
3. NSSO, Employment and Unemployment Surveys, various rounds.

In spite of the slackening of growth in 1999-00, the second period had a much higher growth of Net Domestic Product (NDP[3]), 6.4 compared to 5.7 per cent (point-to-point estimates) in the first period.[4] We have also computed growth rates for NDP using the trend rate and tested for the significance in growth using the dummy variable test. The trend growth rates are similar to point-to-point estimates implying that the growth rates are not influenced by the choice of the reference year. The rate of growth in the second period, 1993-4 to 1999-00, is significantly different from the first period for total NDP, agriculture and non-agriculture (Table 2). Thus the test of regime analysis (dummy variable test) confirms the significantly higher growth in the post-reform period compared to the pre-reform period.

Growth of NDP in the non-agricultural sector was much higher in both periods, and increased from 6.4 to 7.8 per cent in the two periods. Hence there was a sharp rise in the growth of the non-agricultural sector, overshooting the overall GDP growth of 6.4 per cent in 1993-4 to 1999-00. There was a slight decline in the growth of employment in non-agriculture from 3.3 to 2.7 per cent. The fall in overall growth of employment was mainly due to the drastic fall in employment growth in the agricultural sector. The rapid increase in GDP with a fall in growth of employment in the reforms period led to a large increase in growth of labour productivity both in total and non-agricultural sectors.

SHARE OF THE UNORGANIZED SECTOR IN GDP AND EMPLOYMENT

A recent Task Force on Employment Opportunities set up by the Planning Commission (2001) in India pointed out two structural features of the employment situation in India that made the situation in this country different from others. The first is the distinction between the organized and unorganized sectors and the second is between wage and self-employment. Large proportions of the workforce are engaged in the unorganized sector and are self-employed, as we shall see below.

A picture of the aggregate growth of the economy in India in terms of output, employment and productivity can be misleading due to the structural features presented above. A large proportion of the workforce is in the unorganized sector. These workers are engaged in

TABLE 3. SHARE OF UNORGANIZED SECTOR IN NON-AGRICULTURAL GDP AND EMPLOYMENT

	1983	1987-8	1993-4	1999-2000
NDP	49.3	47.0	46.8	45.1
Employment	76.1	78.7	80.9	83.5

SOURCES: Same as Table 2.

economic activities with lower productivity resulting in lower incomes. They are also engaged in activities with less stable employment contracts (including the self-employed) and fewer social security benefits. While the wages and salaries of the formal sector workers are revised periodically to counter inflation, no such benefits accrue to the large proportion of workers in the unorganized sector.

The share of the unorganized sector in the non-agricultural gross domestic product and employment are presented in Table 3 for the period 1983 to 1999-2000.[5] The share of the unorganized sector in non-agricultural GDP declined from 49 per cent in 1983 to 45 per cent in 1999-00. The share of the unorganized sector in non-agricultural employment, however, rose from 76 per cent in 1983 to 83 per cent in 1999-00.[6] If one takes the economy as a whole, including the agricultural sector, the share of the unorganized sector in GDP fell from 67 to 60 per cent, while its share in employment remained more or less the same at 92-3 per cent. The unorganized sector is thus absorbing employment at a faster rate than it is generating output compared to the organized sector. This obviously implies a decline in the labour productivity or incomes per worker that the unorganized sector has been generating over the period.

GROWTH OF INCOMES, EMPLOYMENT AND LABOUR PRODUCTIVITY IN THE ORGANIZED AND UNORGANIZED SECTORS

The growth of incomes (NDP), employment and labour productivity in the non-agricultural sector observed during the two periods, is disaggregated into the organized and unorganized sectors (Figures 3 and 4). A sharp increase in the growth of NDP in the organized and unorganized sectors is observed in the second period (Table 4). In the organized sector while non-agricultural NDP growth rose from 7.2 to 8.4 percent, that in the unorganized sector rose from 5.7 to 7.2

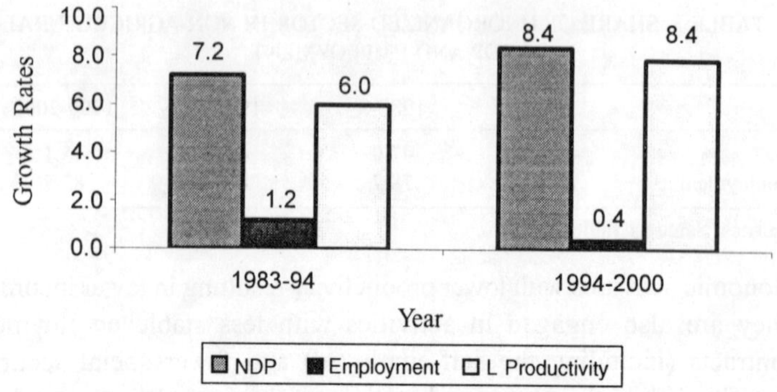

FIGURE 3. GROWTH OF NDP, EMPLOYMENT AND LABOUR PRODUCTIVITY IN ORGANIZED SECTOR (NON-AG).

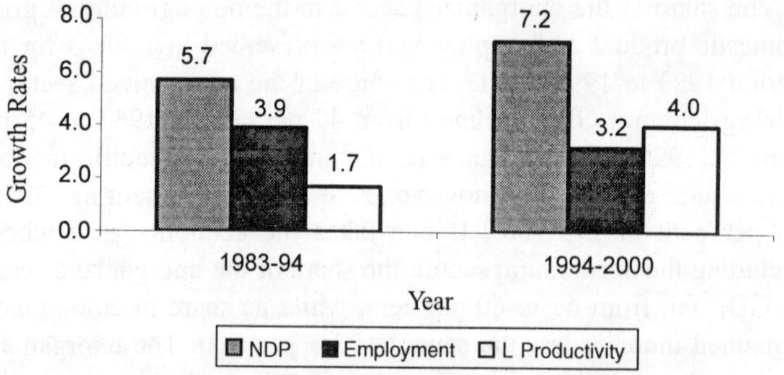

FIGURE 4. GROWTH OF NDP, EMPLOYMENT AND LABOUR PRODUCTIVITY IN UNORGANIZED SECTOR (NON-AG).

percent. While growth in total and organized non-agriculture in the reforms period was significantly different from the pre-reform period that in the unorganized sector was not.

Employment growth was low and declining in the organized sector during the two periods (Table 5). The rapid growth in output, together with low and declining growth of employment, led to a large growth in labour productivity in the organized sector in both periods. In the unorganized sector however employment grew at more than 3 per cent in both periods though at a declining rate after the introduction of reforms. In spite of the large growth of employment, mainly due to rapid growth of NDP, labour productivity growth doubled in the reforms period from nearly 2.0 to 4.0 per cent (Table 6).

This rapid growth of incomes and labour productivity in the unorganized sector points to some positive features of the growth phenomenon since the implementation of the economic reforms. There are perhaps some positive linkages between the organized and unorganized sectors in the economy. It seems that there is a shift of activities from the organized to the unorganized sectors. It is likely that only the high productivity managerial and technologically superior activities are retained in the organized sector, while some of the activities are shifted to the unorganized sectors. Such a shift of activities from the organized sector helps to raise the productivity levels in the unorganized sectors. In the manufacturing sector this could occur through subcontracting out of parts of the production activities by the formal units to smaller units in the unorganized sector. Many service activities such as computing, cleaning and security services may also be contracted out to smaller firms.

GROWTH OF INCOMES, EMPLOYMENT AND LABOUR PRODUCTIVITY BY INDUSTRY GROUPS

Economic policies under the economic reforms could have affected the process of growth differently in the various industry groups. In the manufacturing sector the rate of growth of NDP declined slightly in the organized sector from 6.2 to 5.8 per cent in the reforms period (Table 4). Rate of growth of the manufacturing industry in the unorganized sector, however, rose sharply from 4.1 to 7.4 per cent, during the second period. The decline in growth in the organized sector may be partly due to the recession conditions after 1995-6 leading to large-scale retrenchment from the private sector units and also due to closure of some large public sector units.

In contrast none of the industry groups in the tertiary sector showed any decline in the rate of growth of NDP in the organized sector in the reforms period. The finance industry, however, had exceptionally high growth of NDP in both periods with a slightly lower growth in the second period. Exceptionally high growth was observed in the second period in organized trade, hotels and restaurants industry and in the unorganized transport and communications industry. In order to get some idea of the possible processes at work we concentrate on three contrasting industry groups, manufacturing within the secondary sector and trade, hotels and restaurants and community, social and personal services within the tertiary sector.

TABLE 4. GROWTH RATES OF NDP IN ORGANIZED AND UNORGANIZED SECTORS, 1983-2000

Industry	*Organized*			*Unorganized*			*Total*		
	1983-94	*1994-00*	*1983-00*	*1983-94*	*1994-00*	*1983-00*	*1983-94*	*1994-00*	*1983-00*
Agriculture	1.01	0.66	0.88	4.05	3.07	3.69	3.92	2.99	3.58
Trend growth	-0.92	0.44	0.98	3.49	3.15	4.22	3.31	3.01	4.09
		(2.84)			(2.79)			(2.99)	
Mining & Quarrying	6.81	5.1	6.19	7.96	4.49	6.7	6.89	5.06	6.22
Trend growth	6.02	5.25	7.19	11.03	4.65	8.60	6.39	5.20	7.28
		(2.84)			(-0.74)			(3.68)	
Manufacture	6.21	5.79	6.06	4.14	7.43	5.33	5.40	6.41	5.77
Trend growth	6.55	4.86	6.31	5.75	7.57	5.20	6.23	5.87	5.89
		(0.34)			(-2.78)			(-0.60)	
Electricity, Gas, Water	8.87	8.32	8.67	10.49	2.64	7.64	8.98	7.97	8.61
Trend growth	10.59	8.15	9.00	1.06	3.67	8.55	10.16	7.88	8.97
		(-3.13)			(8.68)			(-2.14)	
Construction	3.69	3.72	3.70	5.93	7.93	6.65	4.77	6.01	5.22
Trend growth	3.08	3.17	3.67	8.18	8.23	6.41	5.64	5.91	5.06
		(1.64)			(-3.77)			(-4.23)	
Trade, Hotels, Restaurants	6.08	16.46	9.85	5.54	7.57	6.27	5.60	8.84	6.77
Trend growth	4.30	16.75	10.83	5.55	7.36	6.35	5.44	8.73	6.93
		(2.10)			(1.25)			(1.78)	
Transport, Storage, Communications	5.62	7.56	6.33	4.52	11.81	7.17	5.13	9.54	6.73
Trend growth	5.82	7.05	6.33	8.46	11.69	5.82	7.17	9.22	6.09
		(0.81)			(-7.13)			(-6.19)	
Finance	13.54	10.88	12.57	11.31	5.19	9.08	12.34	8.24	10.85
Trend growth	13.13	11.05	13.28	3.69	5.30	10.61	8.81	8.40	11.99
		(1.88)			(20.57)			(17.06)	
Community, Social, Personal Services	7.32	8.66	7.81	4.99	6.78	5.64	6.83	8.32	7.37
Trend growth	6.88	8.96	7.52	4.73	6.50	5.66	6.43	8.51	7.15
		(0.32)			(2.20)			(0.65)	
Non Agriculture	7.17	8.35	7.60	5.66	7.21	6.23	6.44	7.83	6.94
Trend growth	6.99	7.98	7.74	5.93	7.40	6.60	6.48	7.71	7.20
		(2.61)			(1.50)			(2.25)	
Total NDP	6.61	7.78	7.04	5.19	5.51	5.31	5.69	6.38	5.94
Trend growth	6.21	7.19	7.09	4.92	5.78	5.69	5.38	6.31	6.21
		(2.97)			(2.83)			(3.56)	

NOTES: 1. These estimates are point-to-point estimates of exponential growth and growth rates obtained by fitting a time trend.
2. Figures in brackets are t-statistics for the significance of difference in the trend growth rates between the two periods using a dummy variable.

SOURCES: Same as Table 2.

Manufacturing

In the initial years of planning the organized manufacturing sector was mainly producing basic intermediate goods and machinery as part of the plan to concentrate on heavy industry. There was a clear departure from that strategy in the 1980s with partial liberalization and more so in the 1990s with the introduction of economic reforms. The organized manufacturing industry data (Annual Survey of Industries, ASI) showed that more than half of the growth between 1990-1 and 1997-8 was accounted for by consumer durables (Chaudhuri 2002; Unni et al. 2001). In the 1980s a similar trend is observed, though the contribution of capital goods is higher and that of consumer durables marginally lower than in the 1990s. Further, the strategy of economic reforms in the nineties was crucially dependent on export growth. Both these strategies make growth more volatile since demand for consumer durables is income elastic and export growth is based on international demand. The period till 1995-6, however, did experience a sharp increase in export growth (Lall 1999).

As observed earlier the rate of growth of NDP in the organized manufacturing sector dropped in the reforms period, but the rate of growth of employment rose marginally. Further, labour productivity in the organized manufacturing sector also declined (Figure 5). While the volatility introduced by the reorganization within the organized sector may account for the decline in rate of growth of NDP, the

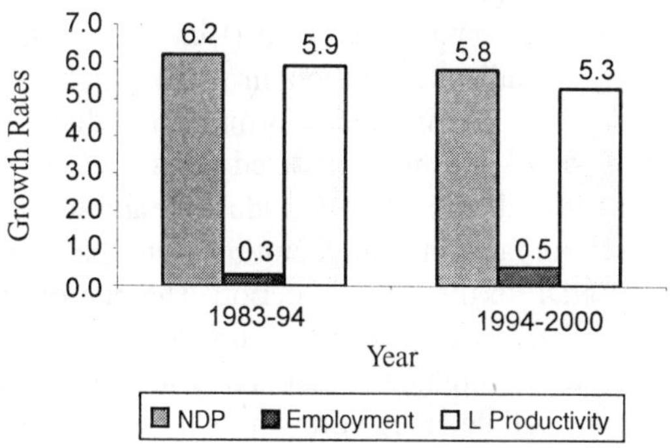

FIGURE 5. GROWTH OF NDP, EMPLOYMENT AND LABOUR PRODUCTIVITY IN ORGANIZED MANUFACTURING.

rapid rise of exports may have led to the marginal rise in employment. Significant growth in employment during 1990-1 to 1997-8 was experienced in textile garments, industrial organic and inorganic chemicals and plastic products (Chaudhuri 2002). According to another study, the gainers in employment growth in the reforms period were chemical industries, textile garments and food products (Tendulkar 2002).

In the organized manufacturing sector the ASI data showed a steady increase in labour productivity from 0.45 in 1990-1 to 0.65 in 1995-6 and stagnation thereafter (Chaudhuri 2002). Labour productivity could increase due to increase in capital productivity. Comparing growth of labour and capital productivity and capital intensity, the study pointed out that while growth of labour productivity was accompanied by some sort of technological upgradation in TV receivers, computers, metal furniture, dairy products, sports goods, pharmaceuticals, motor cycles and scooters, substitution of capital for labour is likely to have occurred in refrigeration, air-conditioners, electrical industrial machinery, weaving and finishing of cotton textiles, motor cars, fertilizers and pesticides, tea, glass products and bicycles.[7]

Overall, the industrial base in organized manufacturing became shallower with growth of consumer durables, the employment situation got worse and labour intensity decreased progressively from 1990-1 to 1997-8 (Chaudhuri 2002), and labour productivity stagnated since 1995-6. The organized manufacturing also saw reorganization in terms of size, with the very large units (above 1000 workers) declining and growth of the middle and small-sized units (Uchikawa 2002). Goldar (2000) observed a small acceleration in employment growth in organized manufacturing during the reforms period due to increase in employment in small and medium-sized private sector factories, which he attributed to liberalization of industrial and trade policies.

In contrast, the unorganized manufacturing sector had a sharp rise in growth rate of NDP in the reforms period. The rate of growth of employment was relatively higher in the unorganized sector in both periods compared to the organized manufacturing sector (Table 5), though there was a small decline in growth in the reforms period and labour productivity rose sharply (Figure 6).

The rapid growth of value added (NDP) and labour productivity in spite of continued high growth of employment in the unorganized

TABLE 5. GROWTH RATES OF EMPLOYMENT IN ORGANIZED AND UNORGANIZED SECTORS, 1983-2000

	Organized			*Unorganized*			*Total*		
Industry	*1983-94*	*1994-00*	*1983-00*	*1983-94*	*1994-00*	*1983-00*	*1983-94*	*1994-00*	*1983-00*
Agriculture	0.76	-0.12	0.44	1.37	-0.13	0.83	1.37	-0.13	0.83
Mining & Quarrying	0.87	-1.73	-0.08	6.31	-3.66	2.68	3.67	-2.83	1.30
Manufacture	0.30	0.52	0.38	2.59	2.02	2.38	2.21	1.80	2.06
Electricity, Gas, Water	2.31	0.15	1.53	18.07	-35.17	-1.29	5.47	-5.96	1.32
Construction	0.24	-0.96	-0.20	6.25	6.84	6.46	5.45	6.20	5.72
Trade, Hotels & Restaurants	1.42	1.08	1.30	3.66	4.49	3.96	3.61	4.44	3.92
Transport, Storage & Communications	0.47	0.34	0.42	4.95	6.91	5.67	3.44	5.28	4.11
Finance	3.36	1.03	2.51	7.17	6.84	7.05	5.37	4.63	5.10
Community, Social & Personal Services	1.76	0.64	1.35	4.73	0.28	3.11	3.63	0.40	2.45
Non Agriculture	1.21	0.42	0.92	3.92	3.24	3.67	3.34	2.74	3.12
Total Employment	1.20	0.35	0.89	2.10	1.00	1.70	2.03	0.95	1.64

SOURCES: Same as Table 2.

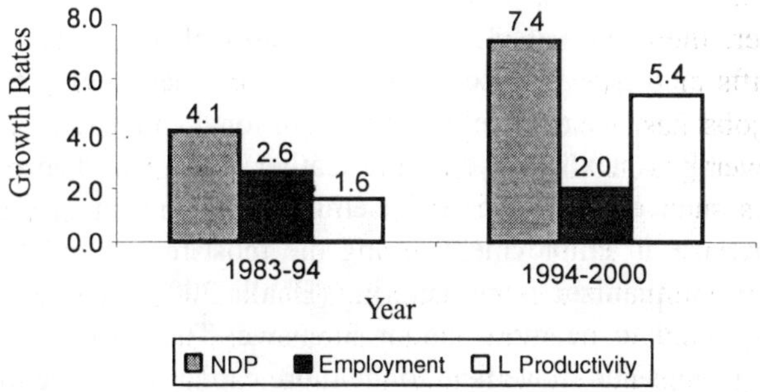

FIGURE 6. GROWTH OF NDP, EMPLOYMENT AND LABOUR PRODUCTIVITY IN UNORGANIZED MANUFACTURING.

sector is a possible sign of positive linkages between the two organized and unorganized sectors. This could lead to a possible convergence in the labour productivity in the two segments as we shall see later. There could be two reasons for this possible convergence.

The activity mixes in the organized and unorganized sectors within the manufacturing industry could be changing. As we observed for the case of the economy as a whole, it is likely that only the high productivity managerial and technologically superior activities are retained in the organized sector. Some of the production processes in the organized sector are shifted to the unorganized sector. This is mainly done through subcontracting arrangement. This helps to raise the productivity levels of the unorganized sectors and bring it closer to the organized.

A second reason for convergence could be restructuring of the manufacturing industry within the unorganized sector itself. In the process of economic reforms and liberalization the forces of competition are unleashed. This leads to a weeding out of the inefficient, often smaller units. According to the National Sample Survey Organization, Unorganized Manufacturing Sector Survey shows that the total number of enterprises, employment and gross value added (GVA) declined sharply over the period 1984-5 to 1994-5 in self employed enterprises. A decline was observed in the non-directory enterprises (with less than six workers) as well. The larger enterprises (DMEs) however recorded positive growth in number of enterprises, employment and GVA over the entire period, 1984-5 to 1994-5, but a small decline in employment in 1990-5. Thus, the smaller size units tended to decline, more rapidly in rural areas (Unni 2001).

Further, there is a decline in the traditional activities such as handicrafts and artisan based industry. It has been shown that the loss of jobs has been mainly in the traditional industries, such as food, beverages, textiles, wood and leather products. The modern industries, such as electronics and chemical based industries, recorded a net increase in employment during the most recent and difficult period for unorganized manufacturing (Bhalla 2001). The traditional industries tend to be more labour intensive. The decline in these industry groups and movement to the more capital-intensive modern industries could account for the small decline in growth of employment and increase in labour productivity in the latter period. It is likely that the traditional industries are mainly smaller own account enterprises, while the larger enterprises are engaged in the modern manufacturing products. Overall, the smaller enterprises (OAEs) contributed 80 per cent of the employment and 64 per cent of the gross value added. Apparently, there was a restructuring process in unorganized manufacturing sector. The smaller units contracted and the leftover units were more productive. This helped in the process of convergence.

Thus, in the manufacturing sector the story of convergence was a story of the informalization of the production processes and possibly of the labour markets as well. It is a story of the reorganization of size and product mixes in both the organized and unorganized sectors. While smaller units contracted in the unorganized sector a greater proportion of the larger units closed down in the organized sector. Further, some substitution of products and processes in the unorganized sector for those that were earlier conducted or produced in the unorganized sector and to some extent vice versa occurred. This substitution helped in creating positive linkages between the two segments and was beneficial to the growth of the unorganized sector. For example, while the automobile industry developed in the 1990s, many small units manufacturing auto components were set up in the unorganized sector. Further, new export oriented units in the garments and leather industry in the unorganized sector would have also contributed to rapid increase in labour productivity in this sector. Overall, these processes may have helped in the convergence of productivities in the two segments in the manufacturing industry

Trade, Hotels and Restaurants

There was a quantum jump in the rate of growth of NDP in trade and hotel industry in the organized sector in the reforms period from 6.1 to 16.5 per cent. In contrast the unorganized sector grew from 5.5 to 7.6 per cent (Figures 7 and 8). Further, while the rate of growth of employment was minimal in both periods in the organized sector, there was rapid absorption of employment in the unorganized trade and hotels sector at an increasing rate in the two periods (Table 5). The result was a sharp increase in labour productivity in the organized sector from 4.7 to 15.4 per cent and a much smaller increase in the unorganized sector (Table 6).

Kuznets (1974: 95-6) pointed out that faster rise in the share of services sector compared to share of the manufacturing sector was only partly due to the small increase in productivity of labour in several branches of services, but more due 'to the great secular increase in demand. This increase in turn was due partly to the

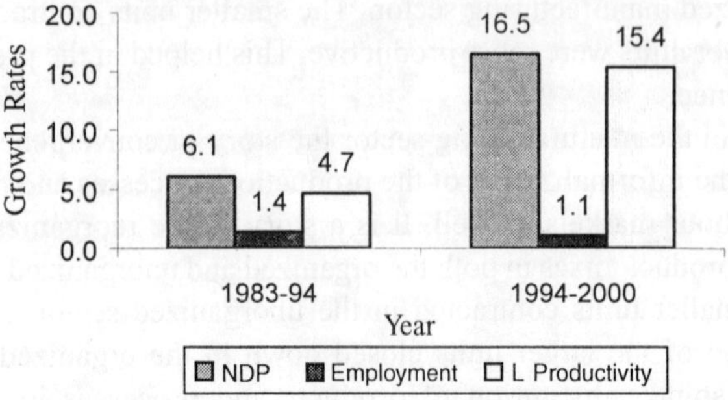

FIGURE 7. GROWTH OF NDP, EMPLOYMENT AND LABOUR PRODUCTIVITY IN ORGANISED TRADE AND HOTELS

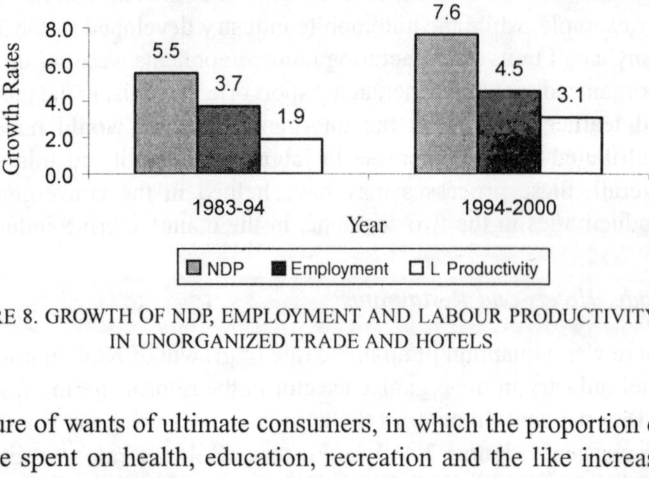

FIGURE 8. GROWTH OF NDP, EMPLOYMENT AND LABOUR PRODUCTIVITY IN UNORGANIZED TRADE AND HOTELS

structure of wants of ultimate consumers, in which the proportion of income spent on health, education, recreation and the like increase with a secular rise in income per capita; partly to the changed condition of life (urbanization) which increased the need for services; and partly to the demands of the developing productive organization of commodity output for more transportation, communication, trade, finance, and, not least, government services.'

A recent study has attempted to split the trade ratio (share of trade in GDP at factor cost) into the intermediate and final trade ratios (Datta 2001). The intermediate trade should be determined by the progress of the manufacturing activities, rather than agriculture and services, since it is more likely to be intermediate input-intensive. Final trade ratio would be independent of this relationship. The author

TABLE 6: GROWTH RATES OF LABOUR PRODUCTIVITY IN ORGANIZED AND UNORGANIZED SECTORS, 1983-2000

	Organized			*Unorganized*			*Total*		
Industry	*1983-94*	*1994-00*	*1983-00*	*1983-94*	*1994-00*	*1983-00*	*1983-94*	*1994-00*	*1983-00*
Agriculture	0.25	0.78	0.44	2.67	3.20	2.86	2.55	3.12	2.76
Mining & Quarrying	5.94	6.83	6.27	1.65	8.15	4.02	3.22	7.89	4.92
Manufacture	5.91	5.27	5.68	1.55	5.41	2.95	3.19	4.60	3.70
Electricity, Gas, Water	6.56	8.17	7.14	-7.58	37.81	8.92	3.51	13.93	7.30
Construction	3.45	4.68	3.89	-0.32	1.09	0.19	-0.68	-0.20	-0.50
Trade, Hotels & Restaurants	4.66	15.37	8.56	1.88	3.07	2.31	1.98	4.39	2.86
Transport, Storage & Communications	5.16	7.22	5.91	-0.43	4.90	1.51	1.69	4.26	2.62
Finance	10.18	9.85	10.06	4.14	-1.65	2.03	6.97	3.61	5.75
Community, Social & Personal Services	5.56	8.03	6.45	0.26	6.51	2.53	3.20	7.93	4.92
Non-agriculture	5.97	7.93	6.68	1.74	3.97	2.55	3.10	5.09	3.82
Total Employment	5.42	7.43	6.15	3.09	4.51	3.60	3.66	5.43	4.30

SOURCES: Same as Table 2.

found that during 1980 to 1995 the rising overall trade services (ratio) was explained by the growth of intermediate inputs trade, which reflected the rise of GDP share of manufacturing and construction sectors. The growth of manufacturing value added was very steep till 1995-6 in both organized and unorganized sectors, and its share rose till 1996-7 (Table 7). This may explain substantial part of the growth of intermediate trade during this period.

In the period after 1996-7, however, there was a decline in the share of manufacturing in GDP, though the share of trade, hotels and services continued to rise (Table 7). This growth in trade services was not led by the growth of manufacturing, but probably consisted of final trade. The demand for final trade services is income driven or the income elasticity of output is very high. A rapid growth of income leads to a rapid growth of a certain quality of services in the organized sector. With the modern lifestyles where work has become very stressful, a new concept of leisure has developed. This is particularly so for the high level professional and managerial staff.

TABLE 7. SHARE OF TRADE, HOTELS AND RESTAURANTS AND MANUFACTURING IN GDP, 1980-2000

Year	*Trade*	*Manufacture*
1980-1	12.19	13.82
1981-2	12.23	14.09
1982-3	12.51	14.58
1983-4	12.23	14.90
1984-5	12.23	15.23
1985-6	12.67	15.15
1986-7	12.85	15.53
1987-8	12.91	16.05
1988-9	12.48	15.81
1989-90	12.60	16.56
1990-1	12.54	16.64
1991-2	12.46	15.83
1992-3	12.58	15.68
1993-4	12.72	16.06
1994-5	13.12	16.76
1995-6	13.99	17.94
1996-7	13.97	18.25
1997-8	14.35	17.68
1998-9	14.41	17.01
1999-00	14.61	17.08

SOURCES: Same as Table 1.

Modern retailing in the form of shopping complexes and multiplexes and the five and four star hotel industry fuelled by the growth of tourism could explain this phenomenal growth in the organized sector. Further, the unorganized trade and hotel industry continued to absorb large proportion of the labour force in the final trade services. The resulting differences in growth of productivity in the organized and unorganized sectors are likely to lead to a divergence in growth of productivity and incomes in the two segments within trade and hotels industry, as we shall see later.

Community, Social and Personal Services

The community, social and personal services was marked by a high growth of NDP in both the organized and unorganized sectors in the second period (Table 4). This sector however, did not absorb much labour in either of the segments in the reforms period (Table 5). The resultant growth in labour productivity was very large in both the organized and unorganized sectors in the reforms period (Table 6).

The gap in incomes and productivity in this sector also did not reduce (Table 8). There is no process of informalization in this sector. In fact a process of formalization seemed more likely. The reasons for this could be many. In the organized sector, services in health and education have shown a large increase (Unni 2001). This is also due to the rise in incomes and an increasing awareness of the need for better health and education in the modern world. Further, part of the increase in incomes and productivity in the organized sector was due to the Fifth Pay Commission increase in incomes.[8] This may not reflect real increases in productivity but definitely implied improved earnings. The unorganized services tends to be more casualized, hence of low productivity and earnings.

LABOUR MARKET OUTCOMES

In an international review of the labour market outcomes noticeable in most developing countries that underwent economic reform, the following was noted: informalization of employment, fall in wage shares and changes in wage distribution (van der Hoeven 2001). Empirically the informalization of the labour force was observed in many countries in Africa, Asia and Latin America (ILO 2002). In Africa this could have been due to the declining number of workers in the state enterprises and lack of generation of employment in the other sectors to absorb the retrenched workers. Another related phenomenon in the period of economic reforms was the increase in wage inequality. In most countries that underwent structural reforms in the 1980s, wage dispersion increased with falling real wages (van der Hoeven 2001).

In India the period immediately after the introduction of reforms saw a very rapid growth of output and labour productivity. However, we noted the structural feature of the existence of a large unorganized sector in India. We have already observed an increasing informalization of the workforce, through the increasing share of employment in the unorganized sector[9] (Table 3). For the benefits of growth to reach a majority of the population it has to percolate to this large and increasing section of the workforce as well. Empirically a convergence of labour productivity and wage earnings in the organized and unorganized sectors would imply declining inequalities and hence percolation of the benefits of growth to the majority.

TABLE 8. DIFFERENTIALS IN LABOUR PRODUCTIVITY AND WAGE EARNINGS, 1983-2000

	Differentials in labour productivity (org/unorg)				*Differentials in urban wage earnings (regular/casual)*			
Industry	*1983*	*1987-8*	*1993-4*	*1999-00*	*1983*	*1987-8*	*1993-4*	*1999-00*
Manufacture	6.3	7.4	10.0	9.9	2.1	1.9	1.9	1.6
Trade, Hotels & Restaurants	5.7	6.4	7.7	16.1	1.5	1.5	1.5	1.8
Finance	0.7	1.0	1.3	2.7	3.6	3.5	4.3	4.0
Community, Social & Personal Services	4.8	6.1	8.4	9.2	3.0	3.1	3.3	5.1
All	3.1	4.0	4.8	6.1	2.3	2.5	2.5	2.9

SOURCES: Same as Table 2.

Labour Productivity and Wage Earnings

We begin with a comparison of the overall labour productivity between the organized and unorganized sectors over the period before and after the introduction of reforms. The absolute level of labour productivity in the organized sector is well above that of the unorganized sector in the economy as a whole. While labour productivity was about Rs. 51,000 in 1983 in the organized sector it was less than Rs. 16,000 in the unorganized sector (Figure 9). Further, while labour productivity rose to Rs. 154,000 in 1999-00 in the organized sector, it rose to only about Rs.25,000 in the unorganized sector. Therefore, while the labour productivity in the organized sector was about 3 times that in the unorganized sector in 1983, it grew to nearly 6 times in 1999-00 (Table 8). Hence, there clearly was a divergence in labour productivity during the period. This could be partly because, other things remaining the same, the capital per worker ratio increased much more in the organized sector compared to the unorganized sector in both manufacturing and services.

The average daily wage earnings of the casual workers in the agricultural and non-agricultural sectors have been shown to rise since the mid-eighties and continued to do so even in the nineties (Sundaram 2001). This together with the decline in proportion of population below the poverty line has been taken as a sure sign of the beneficial impact of economic reforms and the resulting growth.

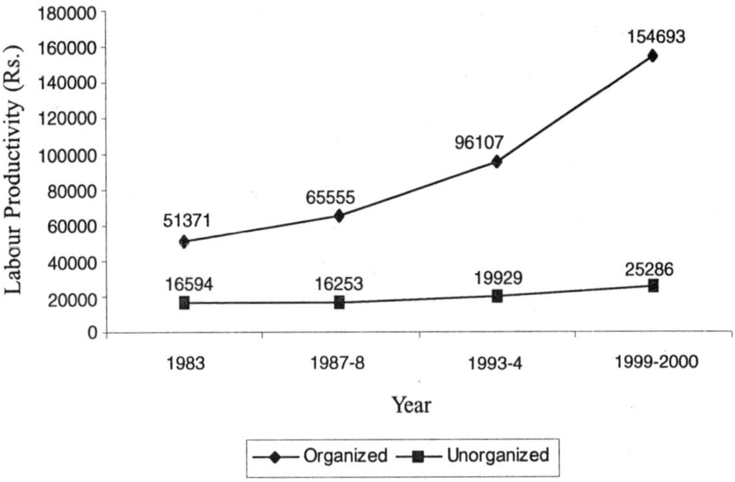

FIGURE 9. DIVERGENCE OF LABOUR PRODUCTIVITY.

However, the divergence of labour productivity observed above, points to a possible increase in the wage inequalities or divergence of wages to different status and skill categories of workers. If the benefits of growth are to really percolate to the bottom sections of the labour market, the wage differentials should decline.

Within the non-agricultural sector there are regular workers and casual labourers. The regular workers may belong to either the organized or unorganized sectors, but constitute a category of workers with more stable contracts. Such workers can be considered to belong to different skill categories as well, with the majority of regular workers having some education or training to warrant the better status compared to the casual workers. The regular workers are assumed to be mainly skilled and semi-skilled workers while casual workers are unskilled workers.

The real wage earnings of both the regular salaried and casual wage workers are seen to increase over the period 1983 to 2000 in both rural and urban areas. However, the earnings rose more rapidly among the regular salaried workers compared to the casual. In fact, the wage differentials have grown over the period from 2.3 to 2.9 in urban areas and from 2.0 to 2.6 in rural areas (Figures 10-11). That is, while wages and salaries of the regular workers were about 2.3 or

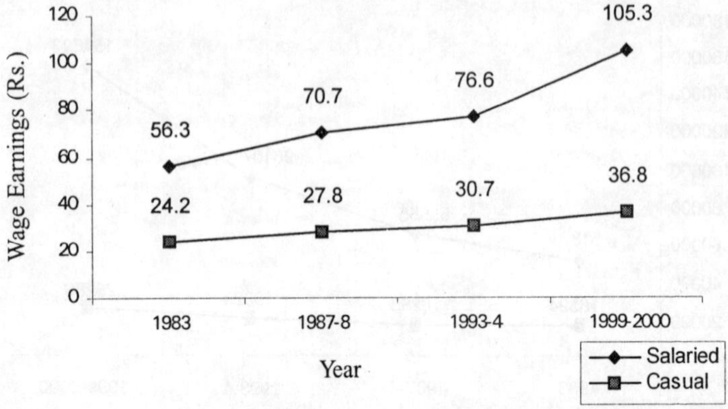

FIGURE 10. DIVERGENCE OF WAGE EARNINGS (URBAN).

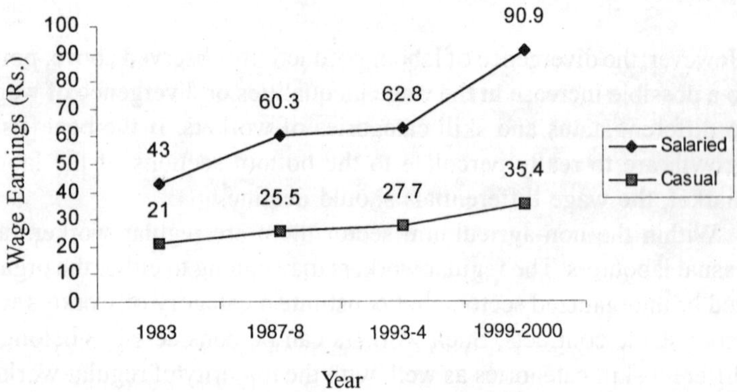

FIGURE 11. DIVERGENCE OF WAGE EARNINGS (RURAL).

2.0 times higher than that of the casual workers in 1983, the differential grew to 2.9 or 2.6 times in 1999-00 in urban and rural areas respectively. Thus, there has not been any catching up of earnings of the casual workers, mainly engaged in the unorganized sector and regular workers, mainly engaged in the organized sector, during this period.

Labour Productivity and Wage Earnings in the Manufacturing and Trade Sectors

In the analysis of growth of incomes, employment and labour productivity we had observed different patterns in the manufacturing and trade sectors. We shall now look at the differentials in productivity and earnings in the two sectors as well.

In the organized manufacturing sector, the labour productivity grew from Rs. 55,000 in 1983 to Rs. 1,41,000 in 1999-00. While labour productivity was at a low of Rs. 8,700 in the unorganized sector in 1983, it rose to only Rs.14,000 in 1999-00 (Figure 12). The differential in labour productivity thus rose in the two sectors in manufacturing from about 6.3 to 9.9 during the period. In contrast the divergence in labour productivity was much greater in the trade sector over the period (Figure 13). In 1983, labour productivity was nearly 5.8 times greater in the organized sector compared to the unorganized. In 1999-00, however, the differential rose to about 16 times (Table 8).

We were able to obtain the disaggregated earnings data by industry groups only for the urban workers. We observed an interesting difference in the urban wage differential between the manufacturing and trade sectors. In the manufacturing sector while the earning of regular workers was 2.1 times higher than that of the casual workers in 1983, the differential declined to 1.6 in 1999-00 (Table 8 and

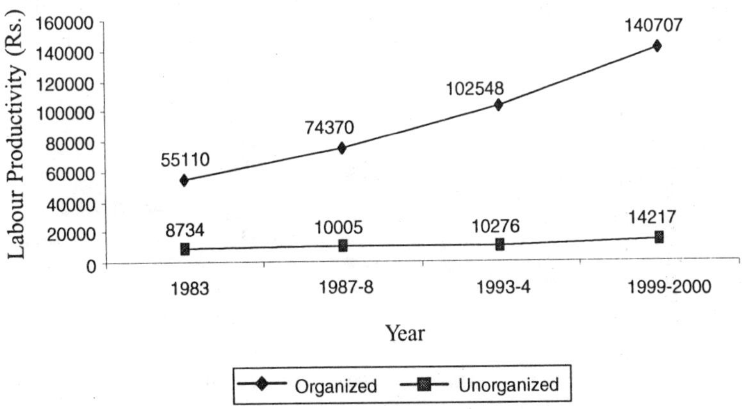

FIGURE 12. DIVERGENCE OF LABOUR PRODUCTIVITY IN MANUFACTURING.

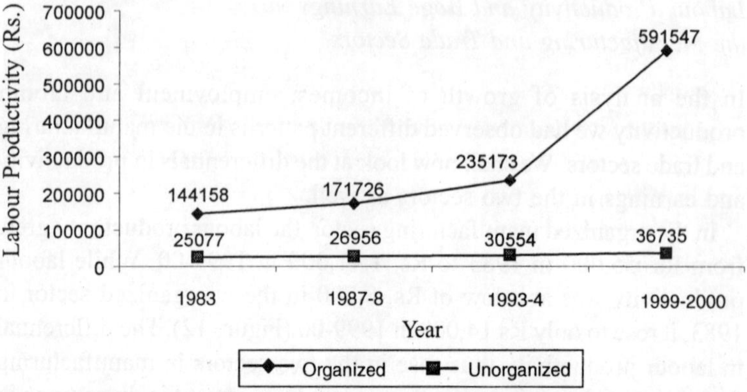

FIGURE 13. DIVERGENCE OF LABOUR PRODUCTIVITY IN TRADE.

Figure 14). Hence there was a convergence of wage differential in the manufacturing sector. The wage earnings in organized trade sector were 1.5 times higher than that in the unorganized segment in 1983. This differential, however, rose in 1999-00 to 1.8 times (Figure 15). Hence the very rapid growth of output and labour productivity in organized trade and the sharp increase in labour productivity differentials in the recent years is clearly reflected in the increasing wage differential as well in this industry group.

Positive linkages between the organized and unorganized segments in the manufacturing sector along with restructuring within them perhaps led to relatively greater convergence in productivity and

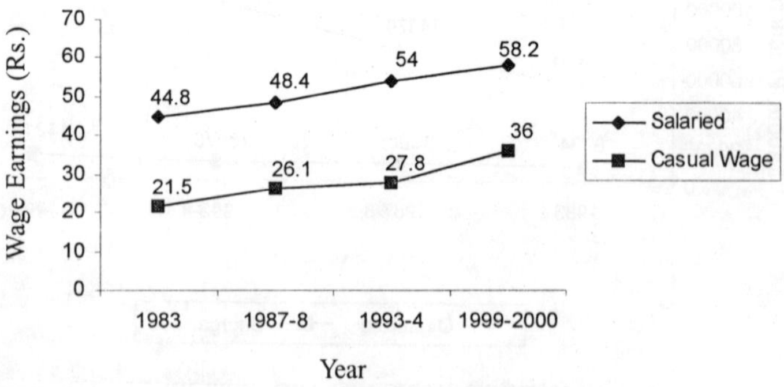

FIGURE 14. DIVERGENCE OF URBAN WAGE EARNINGS, MANUFACTURING.

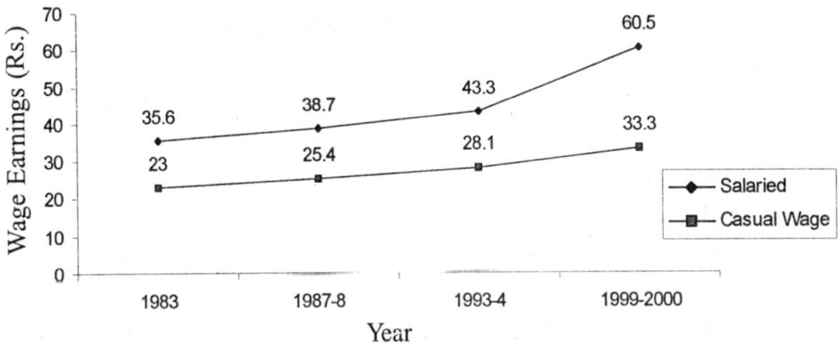

FIGURE 15. DIVERGENCE OF URBAN WAGE EARNINGS, TRADE.

earnings in the manufacturing compared to the trade and hotels sector. Hence, at least a part of the benefits of the growth and increase in labour productivity are reflected in the decline in wage earnings differentials in the manufacturing sector. The rapid growth of output and productivity in the trade and hotels sector, however, led to further dispersion and inequality within the trade sector. The benefits of growth were less evenly distributed in this industry group.

CONCLUSIONS

The period after the introduction of economic reforms was a period of rapid growth in the Indian economy. In more recent years, however, recessionary conditions are being felt in the economy. Since 1995-6 the growth of the tertiary sector has actually helped to buoy up the growth of GDP while recession in the economy hit mainly the manufacturing industry. In such a situation the growth of final trade services and entertainment services such as modern retailing, hotels and tourism related services and other services like education and health become important. These economic activities are not dependent on the manufacturing sector and have a logic of growth of its own.

A dynamic element was introduced in the economy with reforms in an effort to achieve more flexibility in the system. The introduction of flexibility in the labour market led to some displacement of labour and an informalization of the labour force. The impact of economic reforms on the informal sector is two fold. Firstly, workers in the formal sector lose jobs and move to the informal sector. These workers could be part of those that bear 'the real brunt of adjustment'

(Nagaraj 2002), that is loss in wages and social security benefits. A second process is the effect on the informal sector workers that could be positive or negative. These workers may gain from the shift of jobs from the formal to the informal sector in terms of higher wages and productivity. This would help in the process of convergence. The informal workers, however, may loose due to further reduction in wages and even in employment.

We observed increasing divergence in the labour productivity and earnings in the aggregate. Thus, overall there was an increase in differentials in both labour productivity and earnings indicating deteriorating labour market conditions in the economy as a whole.

The story was, however, not uniform in the economy. In the manufacturing sector some positive linkages were observed between the organized and unorganized sectors. This possibly led to relatively less divergence in labour productivity and increasing convergence of wage differentials in the recent period. This provides some preliminary evidence that the benefits of growth were better distributed between the organized and unorganized segments in the manufacturing sector. The industry groups within the tertiary sector however, did not show any evidence of such convergence. Modern trade, hotels and other service industries in the organized sector did well in the reforms period, to the exclusion of the unorganized sector.

NOTES

1. It has been argued that the shocks in agriculture cause shocks in both the private non-agricultural sector, through expenditure, and exports, through agricultural products (Morris 1997). To what extent this link can be broken in India with such a large proportion of the population still dependent on agriculture needs further investigation.
2. Data on gross domestic product is used as a proxy for the growth of income. Data on employment is obtained from the Employment and Unemployment Surveys of the National Sample Survey Organisation (NSSO). While time series data on GDP are available, data on employment are available only every five years, that is 1983, 1987-8, 1993-4 and 1999-00. The cut-off point of 1993-4 is based on the NSS Employment-Unemployment data.
3. The later analysis is focused on the organized and unorganized sectors. The break-up of national product by organized and unorganized sectors is obtained

only for the Net Domestic Product, that is, Gross Domestic Product minus depreciation. Hence these growth rates are also calculated for the NDP.

4. Nagaraj (2000) argued that there is no significant difference in the rate of growth of GDP between the pre-reform (1980-1 to 1990-1) and post reform (1990-1 to 1999-00) periods. Using a similar dummy variable test we also found that there is no significant difference in the trend growth rate of GDP in the two periods. However, when we did an F-test to test for a significant difference in growth rate and variability in the two periods we get a significant result. If the growth rates are not significantly different, as obtained from the t-test, the F-test implies that the variability in growth over the two periods is different leading to a significant difference in the growth rate in the two periods. Further, when we change the periods to 1983 to 1992-3 and 1993-4 to 1999-00, both the t-test and F-test confirm that the growth rate in the post-reform period is significantly higher than in the pre-reform period.
5. In India, the National Accounts Statistics (NAS) has a clear and practical definition of the organized sector. The organized sector units are enterprises in the public (government) sector, private corporate sector and cooperatives, manufacturing units registered under the Indian Factories Act, 1948 or the Bidi and Cigar Workers Act, 1966 and recognized educational institutions. Enterprises that do not belong to any of these categories are unorganized sector units.
6. This estimate of employment in the unorganized sector is obtained by the residual method. The estimate of the total workforce in each reference year is obtained by applying the workforce participation rates of the Employment and Unemployment Survey of the NSS on the population interpolated for the inter-censal years. This estimate and the industrial distribution of the workforce in the NSS are used to arrive at the estimates for the total workforce in the one-digit industry group. Estimate of employment in the organized sector from the Directorate General of Employment and Training (DGE&T), Ministry of Labour, has been subtracted from this estimate of the total workforce to obtain employment in the unorganized sector by industry-group.
7. Chaudhuri (2002) argues, 'With a rise in capital intensity, if capital productivity declines substantially, then it is likely that there has been merely substitution of capital for labour.' However, it has been pointed out by Shuji Uchikawa that this argument neglects the possibility of under-utilization of capacity. If utilization of capacity declines after a firm introduces capital-intensive higher technology, value added against capital stock may drop.
8. Part of the increase in incomes in the services sector is spurious and results from the higher pay scales due to the Fifth Pay Commission decision. The Pay Commission effects are spread mainly over the three years 1997-8, 1998-9 and 1999-00 (Acharya 2002). This impact is felt in the organized sector and widens the gap between organized and unorganized sectors.
9. The process of informalisation has been going on for a longer period and predates the introduction of economic reforms (Ghose 1999). We computed an Employment Quality Index, similar to the one computed by Ghose, and observed that while this was stagnant between 1987-8 and 1993-4 it deteriorated only slightly after 1993-4.

REFERENCES

Acharya, S., 2002, 'India's Medium Term Growth Prospects', *Economic and Political Weekly*, 37(28).

Chaudhuri, Sudip, 2002, 'Economic Reforms and Industrial Structure in India', *Economic and Political Weekly*, 37(2).

Bhalla, Sheila, 2001, 'Assessing the Quality of Employment Growth Using National Sample Survey Data', paper presented at the Golden Jubilee Seminar on Understanding Human Development through National Surveys, Pune, March.

Datta, Madhusudan, 2001, *The Significance and Growth of the Tertiary Sector: Indian Economy 1950-97*, Northern Book Centre, New Delhi.

Ghose, A.K., 1999, 'Current Issues of Employment Policy', *Economic and Political Weekly*, 34(36).

Goldar, B.N., 2000, 'Employment Growth in Organized Manufacturing Sector', *Economic and Political Weekly*, 35(14).

van der Hoeven, R., 2001, 'Labour Markets and Economic Reforms under the Washington Consensus: What Happened to Income Inequality?', *The Indian Journal of Labour Economics*, 44(3).

ILO, 2002, *Women and Men in the Informal Economy: A Statistical Picture*, Employment Sector, International Labour Organization, Geneva.

Killick, Tony (ed.), 1995, *The Flexible Economy: Causes and Consequences of the Adaptability of National Economies*, Routledge, ODI, London.

Kuznets, S., 1974, *Economic Growth and Structure: Selected Essays*, Oxford and IBH Publishers Co., New Delhi.

Lall, Sanjaya, 1999, 'India's Manufactured Exports: Comparative Structure and Prospects', *World Development*, 27(10).

Morris, Sebastian, 1997, 'Why Not Push for a 9 Per Cent Growth Rate?', *Economic and Political Weekly*, 32(20-1).

Nagaraj, R., 2002, 'Performance of India's Manufacturing Sector in the 1990s: Some Tentative Findings', in S. Uchikawa (ed.), *Economic Reforms and Industrial Structure in India*, Manohar, New Delhi.

Nagaraj, R., 2000, 'Indian Economy since 1980: Virtuous Growth or Polarisation', *Economic and Political Weekly*, 35(4 August).

Planning Commission, 2002, *Report of the Task Force on Employment Opportunities*, Government of India, July.

Stiglitz, Joseph, 1998, 'Towards a New Paradigm for Development: Strategies, Policies and Processes', Prebisch Lecture at UNCTAD, Geneva.

———, 2000, 'Democratic Development as the Fruits of Labor', Keynote address to the Industrial Relations Research Association, Boston, January.

Sundaram, K. 2001, 'Employment and Poverty in 1990s: Further Results from NSS 55th Round Employment-Unemployment Survey, 1999-2000', *Economic and Political Weekly*, 36(32).

Tendulkar, Suresh, 2002, 'Employment Growth in Factory Manufacturing Sector during pre and post reforms Periods', Delhi School of Economics' (unpublished).

Uchikawa, Shuji, 2002, 'Employment in the Manufacturing Organized Sector in India: The Rise of Medium Scale Units', companion paper in the current volume.

Unni, Jeemol, 2001, 'Gender and Non-farm Employment in India', paper presented at the Workshop on Rural Transformation in India: The Role of the Non-farm Sector, organized by the Planning Commission, DFID, UK, The World Bank and Institute of Human Development, New Delhi, 19-21 September.

Unni, Jeemol, N. Lalitha and Uma Rani, 2001, 'Economic Reforms and Productivity Trends in Indian Manufacturing', *Economic and Political Weekly*, 36(41).

Employment and Human Resource Practices in Public Sector Banks in the 1990s

ERROL D'SOUZA

1. PERFORMANCE AND THE STRUCTURE OF EMPLOYMENT

The reforms of the financial sector in India have been guided by the report of the Narasimham Committee which was issued in November 1991. These reforms aimed at improving the efficiency of the banking system, introducing transparency in operations, and ensuring that the sector is operating on a sound financial footing. The Narasimham Committee drew attention to the poor loan recovery, weak capital position, high cost and low profitability of public sector banks and attributed this not to public ownership but pointed instead to the managerial and policy environment within which banks had operated (Bery 1994). On this basis controls on interest rates were removed, the pre-emption of bank assets were reduced, and regulatory and supervisory standards were strengthened. The new norms of asset classification, income recognition, and capital adequacy requirements that were introduced resulted in many public sector banks reporting losses—as a group these banks reported a net loss of Rs. 3,293 crore in 1992-3 and Rs. 4,349 crore in 1993-4—and the non-performing loans of these banks were found to be about 21 per cent of their loan portfolio in 1992-3.

The public sector banks, however, constitute two sets of banks. The State Bank of India (SBI) and its seven associate banks were the only public sector banks from 1955 to 1969 when the Nationalization Act nationalized the 14 largest private sector banks and another 6 banks were nationalized in 1980.[1] The 27 public sector banks dominate the commercial banking sector with a share of 87.2 per cent of assets in 1992-3 and 79.7 per cent in 1999-2000. 91.3 per cent of the bank branches in the country in 1992-3 and 89.8 per cent of the branches in 1999-00 belonged to the public sector banks. About 65.8 per cent of these branches of the public sector were in rural and semi-urban areas. By contrast, 57.2 per cent of the private sector bank branches were in rural and semi-urban areas whereas foreign banks had no presence at all in these areas with all their branches located in urban and metropolitan areas.[2] The expansion of private sector and foreign banks was strictly regulated and only since 1993 have new private and foreign banks been allowed to enter the market. Currently there are 32 private sector banks (8 of them having set up since April 1994) and 42 foreign banks operating in India.

The performance of the domestic private and foreign banks has been stronger than that of the public sector banks. Many explanations have been advanced for this phenomenon ranging from them not having the burden of a large network of branches especially in low diversity business areas such as in rural areas, they have been able to introduce technology to upgrade operational efficiency, and their business strategy has concentrated more on high yielding fee based activities and advisory services. The non-performing assets of public sector banks have been considerable. At the end of 1999-00, the net NPAs of public sector banks were 7.60 per cent of advances for public sector banks (7.22 per cent for the SBI group), 4.58 per cent for the private banks, and 2.12 per cent for the foreign banks. Five public sector banks—State Bank of Bikaner & Jaipur, Indian Bank, Allahabad Bank, United Bank of India, and Dena Bank—had particularly high levels of NPAs over 10 per cent of advances, whereas six private sector banks—the Catholic Syrian Bank Ltd., the Nedungadi Bank Ltd., the Dhanalakshmi Bank Ltd., the Benares State Bank Ltd., Lord Krishna Bank Ltd., and SBI Commercial & International Bank Ltd.—had similar NPA-advances ratios. As regards capital adequacy, the minimum prescribed capital to risk-weighted assets ratio was raised to 9 per cent from the year ended March 2000 and only one nationalized bank—Indian Bank—and three private banks—the Bank of Rajasthan Ltd., the Catholic Syrian Bank Ltd., and the Benares State Bank Ltd. did not meet this criterion.

The performance of the commercial banks is given in Table 1. The profitability of the public sector banks in the decade of the 1990s was much lower than that of private sector banks and foreign banks. Net profits as a percentage of working funds[3] was 0.21 per cent for the decade of the nineties for the public sector banks as a whole. The

TABLE 1. NET PROFITS AND ESTABLISHMENT EXPENSES

	SBI & associates	*Nationalized banks*	*Private sector*	*Foreign banks*	*SBI & associates*	*Nationalized banks*	*Private sector*	*Foreign banks*
	Net profit as % of working funds				*Establishment expenses as % of total expenditure*			
1990-1	0.17	0.16	0.37	1.54	21.29	18.75	26.01	7.48
1991-2	0.21	0.33	0.57	1.58	15.26	16.84	20.88	5.51
1992-3	0.22	-1.71	0.35	-2.91	17.27	15.05	18.62	4.42
1993-4	0.25	-1.98	0.57	1.52	18.58	15.21	16.94	7.87
1994-5	0.54	0.10	1.16	1.70	21.45	20.28	16.88	8.37
1995-6	0.43	-0.36	1.19	1.46	21.84	19.95	13.78	8.62
1996-7	0.82	0.41	1.13	1.20	20.15	19.92	10.92	8.53
1997-8	1.04	0.62	1.04	0.96	20.82	19.75	9.86	7.65
1998-9	0.51	0.37	0.68	0.77	19.70	19.59	9.71	8.58
1999-00	0.80	0.44	0.90	1.17	18.91	19.17	9.61	9.28
Average	0.58	0.00	0.89	0.94	19.62	18.74	11.84	7.92
Average 1995-00	0.72	0.33	0.94	1.08	20.13	19.63	10.34	8.55

SOURCE: IBA (1999, 2001).

State Bank group did better, returning a figure of 0.58 per cent for the decade whilst the figure for the nationalized banks was 0 per cent. These figures for the public sector banks is much lower than the 0.89 per cent for private sector banks and 0.94 per cent for foreign banks. The net profits of the nationalized banks were negative in 1992-3 and 1993-4 as they had to adopt the new norms of asset classification and income recognition. In the latter half of the decade the performance of the public sector banks improved—the net profits as a percentage of working funds for the public sector banks went up by 124 per cent to 0.48 per cent—the SBI group returned 0.72 per cent and the nationalized banks 0.33 per cent in the latter half of the 1990s. The performance of the private sector banks and foreign banks did not improve as rapidly in the latter half of the nineties—the ratio of the profitability of private and foreign banks together to all public sector banks was 4.29 for the decade of the 1990s but this halved to 2.10 for the latter half of the 1990s.[4]

The source of this improved relative profitability can be investigated by examining the components of the profitability ratio. Net profits increase as long as the growth of net interest income plus other income (commission, exchange and brokerage, etc.) exceeds the growth of operating expenses and expenditures on provisioning (including contingencies). On the other hand, the growth of working funds is driven by the growth of deposits, borrowings, and other liabilities. Hence, profitability as measured by the ratio of net profits to working funds increases with an increase in (1) net interest income, and (2) other income; and decreases with an increase in (1) operating expenses, (2) provisions, and (3) any component of working funds such as deposits. For the latter half of the nineties[5] it turns out that in the private and foreign banks the growth of net interest and other income was higher than that of the SBI group and nationalized banks—Table 2. Despite this, the relative profitability declined due to the very large growth rates of their operating expenses and provisions. For the private and foreign banks combined the growth rate of operating expenses was 18.82 per cent in the latter half of the nineties compared to 10.32 per cent for all the public sector banks. Similarly, the growth rate of provisions for the private and foreign banks combined was 16.33 per cent, much above the 2.47 per cent of the public sector banks. In addition, the growth rate of working funds (deposits) of the private and foreign banks combined was 27.02 per cent (21.77 per cent), higher than that of the public sector banks' figure of 14.58 per cent (16.18 per cent).

There are three implications that derive from the data in this Table. First, the growing asset base of the private and foreign banks means that they are increasingly able to attract deposits away from the public sector banks despite the large number of bank branches that public sector banks have. In 1995-6, the public sector banks' share of total

TABLE 2. GROWTH RATES OF COMPONENTS OF PROFITABILITY, 1995-2000

	SBI & associates	*Nationalized banks*	*Private banks*	*Foreign banks*
Net Profits	23.05	16.98	16.32	9.25
Working Funds	15.13	15.15	27.02	14.30
Deposits	17.80	15.55	27.84	11.87
Net Interest Income	9.32	11.72	16.22	13.07
Other Income	9.01	14.48	26.19	15.83
Operating Expenses	9.70	10.69	19.87	17.83
Provisions & Contingencies	1.59	3.24	23.64	11.66

SOURCE: IBA (1999, 2001).

deposits raised by commercial banks was 85.43 per cent whereas by 1999-00 it had declined to 81.9 per cent. Also, private and foreign banks were increasingly able to raise these deposits at more favourable net interest rates—their share of net interest income which was 16.99 per cent in 1995-6 improved to 20.23 per cent by 1999-00. Second, the private and foreign banks have been aggressive in making expenditures that are provisioning and contingency related. This reflects possibly more sound risk-management practices and given that their capital adequacy ratios have been much higher it has contributed to making them safer financial intermediaries, thereby enabling their borrowing at lower interest rates, which contains their interest expenses. The relatively lower profitability of the private and foreign banks is therefore a result of more prudence in management and that is a tradeoff taken which needs to be part and parcel of any judgement about declining growth rates of profitability. Third, the large growth rate of operating expenses by the private and foreign banks would seem to point to their being high cost operators. However, investigation of their operating expenses shows no acceleration in establishment expenses, advertising, insurance, etc., but in other items of expenditure. Here we can conjecture that these banks have been spending heavily on technology upgradation which may have reduced their short-term profitability but which will improve their longer-term returns as they leverage the technology to provide better customer support and to manage their assets. Due to these three considerations, the improved relative profitability of the public sector banks in the latter half of the nineties is not necessarily reflective of improved performance by these banks.

Banking by its nature is an information (intensive) and human capital-intensive industry. One of the surrogate measures of output of a bank is the net interest income which gets captured in the data on profitability. Another surrogate measure of the output of a bank is the value of deposits and loans that the bank is able to generate. The efficiency of the employees of a bank on this notion can be summarized by the ratio of the deposits plus advances (the turnover) per employee. On this count, the trends in the efficiency of the various types of banks can be gauged from Table 3. Whilst the turnover per employee increased 3.1 times from Rs. 38.49 lakh per employee in 1990-1 to Rs. 122.11 lakh per employee in 1999-00 for the SBI group, it increased 3.1 times for the nationalized banks, 9.3 times for

TABLE 3. TURNOVER (DEPOSITS + ADVANCES) PER EMPLOYEE

(Rs. lakh)

	SBI & associates	*Nationalized banks*	*Private banks*	*Foreign banks*
1990-1	38.49	40.22	27.37	145.32
1991-2	42.99	44.10	35.42	199.49
1992-3	47.28	48.23	43.50	233.03
1993-4	49.61	50.96	55.31	286.39
1994-5	56.59	60.09	73.73	328.19
1995-6	65.67	67.63	100.45	379.53
1996-7	72.51	76.87	131.41	450.79
1997-8	84.43	91.90	168.37	484.22
1998-9	102.45	107.44	193.05	502.75
1999-00	122.11	126.15	255.23	632.15

SOURCE: IBA (1999, 2001).

the private banks, and 4.4 times for the foreign banks during the decade. In 1990-1, the turnover per employee in the private and foreign banks combined was 1.28 times that in the public sector banks. By 1994-5 the multiple was 2.1 times and by 1999-00 it was 2.56 times—i.e. the turnover per employee in the private and foreign banks doubled relative to the public sector banks during the decade. It is true that the public sector banks have a large presence in the rural and semi-urban areas where the foreign banks for instance do not even have a branch. However, even when we compare the turnover per employee amongst banks in urban/metropolitan areas, foreign and private banks are still doing more than twice better than the public sector banks in their ability to mobilize deposits and disburse advances per employee (Anand 2000). A large rural and semi-urban presence of bank branches cannot therefore be an explanation for the much lower operational efficiency of the public sector banks. The trend growth of turnover per employee is 12.5 per cent for the SBI group, 12.8 per cent for the nationalized banks, 25.2 per cent for the private banks, and 15.1 per cent for the foreign banks for the decade.

The superior performance of the private banks is emerging from the performance of the 8 new private banks that have begun operations since 1994. From Table 4, it is evident that for the period 1995-6 to 1999-00 the growth in turnover was highest for the private sector banks at 25.8 per cent. However, even though the old private sector banks' turnover grew at 18.4 per cent—a slightly faster rate than that of the SBI group where turnover growth was the second fastest—

TABLE 4. TREND GROWTH RATES OF TURNOVER AND EMPLOYEES, 1995-6 TO 1999-2000

(%)

	Turnover	*Employees*
SBI & Associates	16.00	0.14
Nationalized Banks	14.93	-0.89
Private Banks	25.75	3.26
Foreign Banks	11.17	-0.12
Old Private Banks	18.42	1.20
New Private Banks	43.84	35.59

SOURCE: IBA (1999, 2001).

the new private banks' turnover growth was significantly higher at 43.8 per cent. The growth of employment in the new private banks was also significantly higher but this is to be expected given that they were setting up operations and establishing their branches. Despite the faster growth in employment in the private banks they were able to achieve an even greater growth of turnover which is attributable to their aggressive concentration on provisioning and technological upgradation referred to earlier which allowed them to reach a wider customer base and to offer a variety of financial services.

In addition, however, there are two dimensions to their employment practices which is indicative of the way human resources are managed in these banks. First, the ratio of establishment costs to total expenditure has been declining in these banks—Table 1—despite their higher growth in employment. In fact, the most drastic decline in the ratio of establishment expenditure to total expenditure has been in the private banks with the ratio reducing from a high of 26.01 per cent in 1990-1 to 9.61 per cent in 1999-00. The establishment expenditures of the private and foreign banks have declined at a faster pace in the latter half of the decade whereas for the SBI group and the nationalized banks there was an increase in their expenditure on establishment in the latter half of the nineties. The establishment expenses as a percentage of total costs of the public sector banks in the latter half of the decade was 19.81 per cent and this was 2.1 times the 9.5 per cent figure for the private and foreign banks combined. The private and foreign banks have thus been able to contain their wages and salaries expenditures compared to the public sector banks despite their higher growth in employment—the productivity of each employee being much higher has contributed to this outcome.

The second distinguishing feature of employment practices in the private and foreign banks is the structural composition of the workforce. Data on employment in commercial banking is given by three categories of employment—officers, clerical staff, and subordinate staff. Amongst commercial banks the employment growth rate from 1990-1 to 1994-5 was 1.21 per cent and this declined to -0.27 per cent during 1995-6 to 1999-00 as they have sought to downsize. The decline in employment growth was sharpest amongst the clerical staff followed by the subordinate staff. For the officers the growth in employment was 1.81 per cent in the first half of the decade and this declined to 0.89 per cent in the latter half of the decade. For the clerical staff, the growth in employment was 0.80 per cent in the first half of the decade and this slipped to -0.89 per cent in the second half of the decade. The growth in employment of subordinate staff also declined substantially from 1.41 per cent in the first half of the decade to –0.34 per cent in the latter part of the 1990s.

The decline in the growth of employment amongst the clerical and subordinate cadres has been concentrated amongst the private and foreign banks—Tables 5A to 5D. For the SBI group and the nationalized banks the ratio of officers, clerical, and subordinate staff to total staff did not show much variation during the decade. For the

TABLE 5-A. COMPOSITION OF EMPLOYEES (PERCENTAGES)—SBI & ASSOCIATES

	Officers	*Clerks*	*Subordinates*
1990-1	25.27	52.16	22.58
1991-2	25.33	51.80	22.87
1992-3	25.46	51.44	23.09
1993-4	25.88	51.58	22.54
1994-5	25.66	51.13	23.21
1995-6	25.54	51.19	23.27
1996-7	25.44	50.90	23.66
1997-8	25.20	50.01	24.79
1998-9	25.29	49.95	24.76
1999-00	25.30	50.07	24.64

SOURCE: IBA (1999, 2001).

TABLE 5B. COMPOSITION OF EMPLOYEES (PERCENTAGES)—
NATIONALIZED BANKS

	Officers	*Clerks*	*Subordinates*
1990-1	27.03	51.13	21.84
1991-2	27.19	51.17	21.63
1992-3	27.21	50.76	22.03
1993-4	27.32	50.08	22.60
1994-5	27.54	50.86	21.60
1995-6	27.86	50.57	21.57
1996-7	28.16	50.90	20.94
1997-8	28.43	50.63	20.94
1998-9	28.80	50.40	20.81
1999-00	28.99	50.33	20.68

SOURCE: IBA (1999, 2001).

TABLE 5C. COMPOSITION OF EMPLOYEES (PERCENTAGES)—
FOREIGN BANKS

	Officers	*Clerks*	*Subordinates*
1990-1	32.06	49.82	18.12
1991-2	35.15	47.99	16.86
1992-3	36.50	47.58	15.92
1993-4	36.49	47.63	15.88
1994-5	39.41	46.71	13.87
1995-6	42.35	45.60	12.05
1996-7	47.73	41.71	10.56
1997-8	52.86	37.36	9.78
1998-9	55.28	34.68	10.04
1999-00	61.14	30.34	8.51

SOURCE: IBA (1999, 2001).

TABLE 5D. COMPOSITION OF EMPLOYEES (PERCENTAGES)—
PRIVATE BANKS

	Officers	*Clerks*	*Subordinates*
1990-1	24.53	54.75	20.72
1991-2	25.09	53.87	21.05
1992-3	25.63	53.44	20.93
1993-4	25.74	53.13	21.13
1994-5	26.72	52.80	20.48
1995-6	29.62	51.53	18.84
1996-7	31.31	50.26	18.43
1997-8	32.91	48.61	18.47
1998-9	34.16	47.47	18.37
1999-00	36.22	45.89	17.88

SOURCE: IBA (1999, 2001).

decade as a whole, for the SBI group, 25.4 per cent of the staff were officers, 51.0 per cent were clerks, and 23.6 per cent were subordinate staff. The composition of staff was the same for the nationalized banks with 27.9 per cent of staff being officers, 50.7 per cent being clerks, and 21.4 per cent being subordinate staff. In the foreign banks and private sector banks, however, there has been growing recruitment amongst the officers' cadre with a decline in the recruitment of clerical and subordinate staff. Private banks started the decade with 24.5 per cent of staff as officers, 54.8 per cent as clerical, and 20.7 per cent as subordinate staff. By the end of the decade 36.2 per cent of the staff were officers, 45.9 per cent were clerical, and 17.9 per cent were subordinate staff. Similarly, foreign banks started (ended) the decade with 32.1 per cent (61.1 per cent) of the staff being officers, 49.8 per cent (30.4 per cent) were clerical, and 18.1 per cent (8.5 per cent) were subordinate staff. The especially noteworthy examples of the staffing pattern tilting in favour of officers is amongst the new private banks—HDFC Bank, Global Trust Bank, UTI Bank, IDBI Bank, for instance, have no clerical and subordinate staff and 100 per cent of the staff in these banks are officers. This is a manifestation of these banks resorting to technology the operation of which requires high-skill human capital for increasing the returns to the technology which anyway enables routine tasks formerly undertaken by lower level staff to be speedily processed. Also the presence of only officers is indicative of multi-tasking which promotes flexibility in the bank and ensures long-term profitability.

Of course, making investments in information technology for banks is a process fraught with opportunities that may not result in a reduction in labour costs but which has the potential of raising revenues. Technology has many benefits in the areas of treasury and asset liability management and in the shape of ATMs as an effective delivery channel as well as a good medium for tapping new customers. Financial intermediaries have been traditionally organized around product lines such as deposit accounts, loans, credit cards, etc. As a result coordination among departments has been loose and customer information does not easily flow across the organization. Those banks that are able to integrate their databases and IT systems are in a position to create a single customer interface which facilitates cross-selling as well as improves customer retention. This boosts the productivity of a bank. Similarly, other IT investments in back-office processes have efficiency enhancing impacts such as check-imaging technology that reduces storage costs as well as check-retrieval time, automated voice response units that reduce call centre representatives and electronic payment transactions that reduce the need for tellers and back-office personnel. However, it needs to be stressed that customization and a wide choice of services that technological investments allow is no substitute for what customers care about most in their interactions with banks—reliability, service, and an institution they can trust.

The increasing pace at which private and foreign banks are reducing their workforce composition away from clerical and subordinate staff and the relative rigidity in the composition of the workforce in public sector banks points to an important distinction between the organization of the private and foreign banks on the one hand and the public sector banks on the other which definitely has an impact on their performance.

The practices of managing human resources at the officers' level are different in the public sector banks and the other banks. The practices regarding compensation, i.e. rules governing pay and pay raises, benefit structures and the practices that centre around training, staffing, hiring and selection, and job design differ substantially. To mention a few differences, public sector banks, structure compensation in such a way that there are lower differentials between employees, long-term tenure is rewarded, and there is a high base pay. In the private and foreign banks there are larger pay differentials, fewer rewards for tenure, and individual incentives are high. Public sector banks place a lot of emphasis on training whereas in the private and foreign banks training is emphasized according to necessity. In terms of staffing the public sector banks are committed to employment security and have a full-time workforce whereas in the non-public sector banks the staffing policy is a hire and fire at will dictated one with a part-time workforce. As regards the practice of hiring and selection public sector banks invest heavily in screening whereas the practices in other banks are more market based. Finally, in terms of the practice of work organization public sector banks have relatively narrow jobs with a steep hierarchy whereas the other banks have broader jobs and a relatively flat hierarchy.

2. HUMAN RESOURCE PRACTICES

To understand the differences in the practices regarding human resource management it is necessary to examine the historical development of the institution of these practices. As Mankidy (2000) observes, in Indian banking, 'from a stage of extreme exploitation of employees prior to the 1940s, the industrial relations process unfolded itself into labour militancy and crises in the 1960s and 1970s. Most of the human resource management practices in the industry, such as salary structure, promotion, transfer, placement, etc. are the by-products of this reactive process.' In the 1940s the management could extract work out of employees as there was a fear of losing the job due to the scarcity of jobs elsewhere. The employees had stretched working hours and low remuneration and there was much discontent with salary and working conditions. A landmark in this period was when the Bank of India Staff Union called the first ever strike which lasted 17 days. This led to the Divatia Award that provided employees with a number of facilities such as a pay scale, annual leave, gratuity, etc., that were hitherto absent. This led to many awards covering bank employees in different states as banks were under state regulation. The passing of the Industrial Disputes (Banking and Insurance Companies) Act in 1949 brought banks under the central government and uniformity in human resource practices began from then onwards. The subsequent disputes between bank employees under the umbrella of the All India Bank Employees Association (AIBEA) and Bank Managements led to a series of prominent awards such as the Sen Award of 1950, Sastry Award of 1953, and Desai Award of 1962. The Industrial Disputes Act allowed for settlements covering only the clerical and subordinate staff and the collective bargaining which started in the early 1960s led to the evolution of a bipartite relationship in the industry. The industry-wise uniformity in service conditions and salary for officers in nationalized banks began with the Pillai Committee Report in 1979.

By the late 1960s unions in banks had become strong and militant. Also, as unionization arose in response to the poor service conditions and low salaries, they fought over issues such as promotion, wages and salaries, welfare measures such as medical facilities and different types of leaves, and over time human resource practices began to be dictated to the banks by the unions. The government in the 1960s and 1970s strengthened the position of workers as the government was guided by the goal of a socialist and equitable society and the role of organized labour since the Independence movement was a strong factor motivating the government's predilection in this regard. This one-sided bargaining process increased the security of employees and their militancy began to decline since the mid-1980s. The liberalization of the financial sector as also the landmark agreement of the SBI management with its union in 1989 on computerization led to the introduction of decentralized bargaining.[6] Besides, employee support for unions began dwindling as evinced by the change from resorting to indefinite strikes to pursue demands to unions calling for only one-day strikes over the last decade due to their lack of confidence over support for longer duration conflicts. Finally, there has also been an attitudinal change amongst unions with their acceptance of the modernization of work practices in the emerging competitive era. The All India Bank Employees Association that had always fought against computerization in October 1993 for instance agreed to signing a Memorandum of Settlement with the Indian Banks' Association that allowed banks to introduce information technology.[7]

The industrial relations structure in the banking industry is such that the management of both the public and private sector banks are organized into one body called the Indian Banks' Association (IBA). There are five major industry level trade unions in banks representing clerical and subordinate staff employees and four associations for officers—see Table 6. Collective bargaining is usually carried out at the industry level between the IBA and mainly the All India Bank Employees Association (AIBEA), the National Confederation of Bank Employees (NCBE) and the Bank Employees Federation of India (BEFI) for issues relating to clerical employees and between the IBA and All India Bank Officers' Confederation (AIBOC) for issues of relevance to officers. In addition, it must be mentioned that the Reserve Bank of India intervenes in human resource practices by issuing various guidelines and instructions keeping in mind government policy as the principal employer of public sector banks and as a continuation of the recommendations of various working groups and committees. RBI instructions have included the setting up of the National Institute of Bank Management in 1968 as an apex institute for training and research, constituting the Banking Service Recruitment Board for recruitment, standardizing performance appraisals

TABLE 6. UNIONS/ASSOCIATIONS/FEDERATIONS IN BANKS

(%)

Clerical and subordinate staff	*Share of membership*	*Officer staff*	*Share of membership*
1. All India Bank Employees Association (AIBEA)	49.49	1. All India Bank Officers Confederation (AIBOC)	73.37
2. National Confederation of Bank Employees (NCBE)	33.62	2. All India Bank Officers Association (AIBOA)	14.93
3. Bank Employees Federation of India (BEFI)	8.10	3. Indian National Bank Officers Congress (INBOC)	6.53
4. Indian National Bank Employees Federation (INBEF)	1.73	4. National Organization of Bank Officers (NOBO)	1.32
5. National Organization of Bank Workers (NOBW)	2.66		

SOURCE: Indian Banks' Association (2000), Indian Banking Year Book, 1999.

for public sector banks from 1993-4, etc. The government is also empowered to issue directives to public sector banks under Section 8 of the Banking Companies (Acquisitions & Transfer of Undertakings) Act 1970/1980 with regard to policy matters involving public interest such as constitutional provisions regarding reservations for socially deprived classes, etc.

The recruitment in public sector banks was standardized with the introduction of the Banking Service Recruitment Boards in 1978-9 by the government. The Narasimham Committee had urged in 1991 to allow banks to make their own officer recruitment more so where special skills were required and to allow clerical recruitment to continue to take place through the Board. The subordinate staff are selected through the local employment exchange. For officers and clerical staff the number of vacancies are determined depending on business growth, branch expansion, existing pattern of staffing and wastages. However, the RBI in February 1990, following up on an earlier Ministry of Finance directive to restrict intake so as to improve productivity, has instructed public sector banks to restrict annual staff growth to 0.75 per cent/1 per cent depending on productivity levels. At lower levels of the job hierarchy banks have the freedom to create additional vacancies, but for additional scale IV and above officer positions prior clearance from the Ministry of Finance is required. The promotion of workers in nationalized banks from subordinate staff to clerk and from clerk to officer is at the discretion of individual banks that have entered into settlements with workers unions. With regard to the intake of employees at the officer level the public sector banks follow a closed system where promotion from within is encouraged. There are mainly two ports of entry into the profession. At the clerical level 75-100 per cent of the vacancies are filled via screening by the Banking Service Recruitment Board and at the Junior Management level 20-5 per cent of vacancies are filled via outside recruitment.

In July 1973 the government had appointed a committee to standardize the pay scales, allowances, and perks of officers. This committee, known as the Pillai Committee, submitted its report in May 1974. The government then appointed a Study Group of Bankers to make suggestions for the implementation of the report which submitted its report in 1977. The Pillai Committee report with the modifications suggested was adopted in 1979 and the Officers' Service Regulation was introduced. The Pillai Committee noted that young recruits tend to get frustrated due to the prevalence of long time scales and the absence of accelerated promotions for the meritorious. The Pillai Committee accordingly suggested seven scales in four grades, i.e. Top Management (2 scales), Senior Management (2 scales), Middle Management (2 scales) and Junior Management (1 scale)—Table 7. The Pillai Committee recommendation of not less than 25 per cent of vacancies in middle and senior management positions to be kept open for merit promotions to enable talented people to reach top positions in the prime of their lives was modified by the Study Group of Bankers who argued that since the executive pyramid is wide based and fairly narrow at the top in banking, the promotion to senior and middle positions should be solely on merit with the years of service required for promotion as suggested by the Pillai Committee being an eligibility criterion on the basis of which selection is to be made with weightages given to objective criteria such as service record, professional qualifications, etc. The Merit Rule thus replaced the Seniority Rule for promotions in middle and senior positions. From the viewpoint of the needs of the bank as opposed to the needs of the individual with regard to non-stagnation, four grades were identified on the basis of differences in levels of

TABLE 7. EXECUTIVE PYRAMID IN PUBLIC SECTOR BANKS

Scale/ Management level grade	*Minimum years of experience before promotion to next grade*	*Competent authority*
Clerks	2-3 years	
I. Junior Management	7 years	1 DGM (Scale VI) 2 AGMs (Scale V)
II. Middle Management	5 years	1 GM (Scale VII) 2 DGMs (Scale VI)
III. Middle Management	5 years	1 CMD/ED 2 GMs (Scale VI)
IV. Senior Management	3 years	CMD, Government, RBI Directors
V. Senior Management	2 years	CMD, Government, RBI Directors
VI. Top Management	2 years	CMD, Government, RBI Directors
VII. Top Management	2 years	
Ports of Entry: (1) Clerical (75-100 per cent)	(2) Junior Management (20-5 per cent)	

responsibility. The Top Management level is conceived as the policy-making level. At Senior Management level there is total responsibility for an entire functional area in the bank such as advances or personnel. The Middle Management level is a support level for higher level managers and a tier for ensuring smooth career progression from an operational job to semi-policy-making areas. The Junior Management level would be involved with operational tasks of a supervisory nature.

As the system of induction, recruitment and promotion operates, it is a case of what has been labelled as an internal labour market (Doeringer and Piore 1971). In the internal labour market the system provides low skill, entry level jobs and the opportunity to learn skills on-the-job along with job ladders for promotion. Given minimally acceptable performance, managerial jobs are till retirement and pay is on the basis of job titles and seniority rather than dependent on individual attributes and is not strictly tied to performance. Internal labour markets are organized around long-term employment relationships so as to enable the capturing of the benefits of the development of skills, especially when they are specific to the firm, as well as allowing the identification of abilities and worker performance in order to fill promotions. The characteristics of an internal labour market can be identified with the following practices—(1) providing own, firm-specific training, (2) an attempt to adhere to the objective of making staff permanent, (3) using internal promotion and job ladders, (4) elaborate and systematic screening and recruitment of employees, and (5) setting wages and salaries according to internal administrative procedures rather than market forces.

The underlying premise of the internal labour market approach is that employees differ in ability—one more unit of effort by different employees implies different productivity for the organization—and there is an information asymmetry in that supervisors have imperfect information about the abilities of the employees. As the ability of the employee is initially unknown, it is only the experience in the employment relationship that allows the employer to learn about such abilities, and as this learning takes place, the employee is placed in more productive jobs. In managerial employment, job changes often imply movements along the hierarchical structure of the firm and are associated with important changes in total salary and remuneration. Current performance is used to evaluate an employee's ability and to decide on future promotions and so current performance affects the rewards earned by the employee.

The promotion to a higher management level is best thought of through the lens of a tournament model (Lazear and Rosen 1981) where the prize in terms of compensation for a position in the hierarchy is fixed in advance and is independent of absolute performance. In effect, an employee is promoted to the next higher level/grade not because he is good, but because he is better than everybody else at the current level/grade—relative performance and not absolute performance matters. A tournament is a mechanism for performing a sorting function—as individuals compete with one another the more able individual gets the promotion and individuals are sorted to their best use. Individual employees are also spurred to exert higher effort due to the higher salary that accompanies the higher position and this is a gain to the organization. Whether a tournament that offers promotions on grounds of merit alone effectively sorts individuals according to abilities and provides adequate incentives in the public sector banks is however a doubtful proposition.

The expected gain to an employee via a promotion equals the probability of promotion multiplied by the increase in the present value of lifetime earnings. In public sector banks the probability of promotion is low due to the large overstaffing. Given that many officers will fail to get promotions in the hierarchy, the Pillai Committee had recommended a single long scale at the base Junior Management level to take care of the career path and sustain the motivation of those who lose out in the tournament. However, the increase in the present value of lifetime earnings is also low in the public sector banks. This is because of the method of pay fixation and the pegging of earnings to the Pay Commission awards. First, there is a pecking order in the financial sector with the RBI which is the regulator and financial institutions that hitherto performed a developmental function being at the top of the pecking order. The State Bank group comes next due to the special function it performs of transacting the government business of both the Centre and the States. Last in the hierarchy are the other nationalized banks. The salary of the Chairman and Managing Director of the banks is fixed by the government keeping in mind parity with the Indian Administrative Service and this then becomes the ceiling on the salary that can be earned in the banks. The subordinate staff, knowing this upper limit, as well as the managerial grades that are operational (seven in all) go into the bargain of their unions such as the AIBEA and NCBE with the IBA with the objective of minimizing the distance between their earnings and that set by the government for the Chairman and Managing Director. As the settlement with the subordinate staff sets the floor for determining officers' salaries, the pay scales for the officers leaves little room for manoeuverability and is sandwiched between the subordinate staff award settlement and the salary of the Chairman and Managing Director. The pay structure that emerges in the public sector banks is therefore compressed and even though the relative responsibility increases significantly as one moves up the organizational hierarchy, the relative increase in compensation does not match up to this increased responsibility. As a result, the use of promotions as they take place currently amongst the public sector banks, is not an effective mechanism for sorting out the higher ability individuals and neither do they provide incentives for increased effort. It is not surprising accordingly that many employees bypass the opportunity for promotion and that with the emergence of the new private banks there is an incentive created for shifting jobs amongst those employees who are less risk-averse and are willing to forego job security.

There are also the more fundamental issues such as that the early years in the management cadre are spent on routine operational functions and as one goes up the ladder the developmental and policy-making roles becomes more important. It could very well be the case that 'the best performer at one level in the hierarchy is not the best candidate in the job one level up' (Baker et al. 1988). The manager who is the best at operations would rarely also be the best at policy-making. That the correlation of the ability to perform in a job with the ability to perform in a job lower in the hierarchy is high is questionable. As a result, employees best suited for top management jobs might lose promotions at lower management levels. Also, promotion systems do not provide optimal incentives if there is a variation in the abilities of individuals and these abilities are revealed over time as this will reduce everyone's incentive given that it is known that only those of high ability will be rewarded with the promotion. Finally, an important part of the compensation of employees in the public sector comes in the form of intangibles which should normally be included as part of the expected total value of the compensation—the quality of the working environment, leisure, relationships with co-workers, and above all, the most important component of the reward—job security. This has the potential of reducing the productivity of those employees who are of low relative ability and as pay is not linked to performance delinks the connection between outcomes for the organization and outcomes for the employees. Whereas job security has the upside that it enables a stable long-term relationship that promotes the capturing of the benefits of firm-specific investments, the downside is that no hiring occurs from outside in the internal labour market and as the abilities of co-employees is known, those who do not expect to have the opportunity to be offered a higher level job will put forth less effort and could even collude to shirk. The organization only rewards relative performance by selecting those few who perform well to move up the executive pyramid but does not reward the absolute performance of those who do not match up to the level of potential promotees, thereby encouraging them to reduce effort and shirk. With time the job motivation of such employees also reduces.

An interesting aspect about compensation policies in public sector banks is that since there is pay compression and so the more able employees' incentives are thereby blunted, one would have expected even larger within job pay for performance such as bonus incentives for incentivizing employees. Promotion rewards can be expected to be more important in fast-growing industries because as those industries grow faster more jobs will be available to feed the reward system. In mature industries competition for market share should be more intense and so promotion opportunities would not grow as rapidly, making it all the more imperative that a variable compensation such as a bonus be used in more concentrated markets. A major part of the reason for the non-existence of these types of bonus payment systems is that banking has been highly regulated which lowers the intensity of rivalry and competition and as socialistic objectives of the decentralization of bank branches became dominant and the major banks were nationalized, profit-maximization no longer became the main criterion of performance. Bureaucratic structures and internal controls began to become the prime concern of managers in nationalized banks. As banks expanded the processes and work organization shifted towards well-structured jobs and standardized procedures which go along with fixed pay compensation policies.

It would be expected that deregulation and increased competition acts as a disciplining force on the operating efficiency of nationalized banks. In the current scenario, whilst banks have considerable discretion over setting of interest rates and on deciding on the product mix, they do not however take full responsibility for their decisions. If they are undercapitalized and run into losses, they face no risk of bankruptcy as government has given an implicit insurance that the stability of the financial system will be maintained—the government's guarantee has in effect imported confidence that less care needs to be taken about the non-marketable, idiosyncratic loans made by banks (D'Souza 2001). The outcome of this is that public sector banks have come to expect support in financial difficulties which reduces their sensitivity to efficiency and shields them from the disciplining force of competition from the non-public sector banks. As a result, even if operational freedom is fully with the public sector banks, and even if the government's stake in the capital of the banks falls to 33 per cent, the management may not operate as efficiently as they possibly could. The situation was reinforced in the Budget Speech 2000 of the Finance Minister when he stated that the 'public nature of the nationalized banks will continue even if the government stake drops to 33 per cent'. The approach adopted of reducing portfolio controls and encouraging the growth of the private and foreign banks was in order to create a more competitive environment with the expectation that this would lead to efficiency improvements.

However, the system of wage negotiations with salaries pegged to comparable levels in government, and without reference to the ability to pay of the banks has inflated the wage bills of public sector banks. It is the implicit government support to ensuring liquidity to the banks that has resulted in employee compensation growing overtime. Moreover, as the risk of bankruptcy is not borne by the bank, this has reinforced the bargain by employees for the payment of higher wages and salaries and severed the link between pay and productivity—as we saw above, establishment costs for public sector banks have been growing in the latter half of the nineties at the expense of provisioning and expenditure on technological upgradation. Thus, despite the presence of newer private banks who are more aggressive in marketing their products as well as provide a greater mix and quality of services, public sector banks have not responded adequately to this competition due to the implicit government support which reduces the risk of bankruptcy and makes the budget constraint of banks appear to be elastic enough to take care of contingencies. This translates into an employee friendly environment where the growth of employee compensation has a greater weightage in decision-making than the growth in profitability.

A related aspect of compensation policy in public sector banks is that pay is compressed relative to the private sector due to the method of pay fixation as was referred to earlier. This has had the effect that public sector banks have found it very difficult to retain motivated employees and their talent pool has been subject to raiding by the private banks. This is also due to talented and not so risk-averse individuals preferring to be rewarded on the basis of performance rather than independent of it. As a result, when the private banks pay more on average and offer stronger pay-for-performance rewards, it is to be expected that talent will migrate to them. Accordingly, the low ability and risk-averse individuals will continue in public sector banks with bureaucratic compensation systems that ignore performance. It has often wrongly been argued that there are important non-monetary rewards that go along with the running of a large organization such as say SBI—power, prestige, and public visibility. However, non-monetary rewards tend to be associated with position or rank in the organization and are fixed thereby reducing the opportunity to link them to performance. As these rewards do not vary with the value of the organization they are not effective in motivating top management from acting in the interests of maximizing the value of the organization and that affects performance.

3. CONCLUSIONS

The profitability of the public sector banks improved in the latter half of the nineties relative to the performance of the private and foreign banks. However, their share of the total deposits raised by commercial banks declined and private and foreign banks were able to attract deposits at more favourable net interest rates. Also, private and foreign banks have been adopting sounder risk management practices and this increased prudence on their part has led to greater expenditures on provisioning which has reduced their profitability. Moreover, private and foreign banks have been investing heavily in technological upgradation so as to provide better customer support and manage assets better. The turnover per employee in the private and foreign banks also improved over the decade and relative to the turnover per employee of public sector banks by the end of the decade it was twice the figure for the beginning of the decade—private and foreign banks improved their efficiency relatively faster during the course of the decade.

The new private banks contributed significantly to the growth in turnover amongst the private banks in the latter half of the decade. And private banks as a whole were able to reduce their establishment expenditures as a ratio of total expenditures drastically in the nineties from 26 per cent in the beginning of the decade to 9.6 per cent by the end of the decade. The downsizing of staff occurred mainly amongst private and foreign banks where the decline in employment was registered mainly amongst the clerical and subordinate cadres—the staffing pattern in these banks tilted in favour of officers during the course of the decade, and multi-tasking became a part of the operations of these banks. The composition of the workforce in public sector banks by contrast is still dominated by the clerical and subordinate staff which constitute three- fourths of the employees which is much larger than in the private and foreign banks. In the public sector banks the power of the unions declined throughout the decade as more decentralized bargaining began to emerge and along with the attitudinal change regarding the acceptance of modern work practices.

The labour market in public sector banks is an internal labour market where the major human resource allocation policy is promotions as there are limited ports of entry and top management positions are decided by merit and the frequency of promotions depends on vacancies. The way promotions are structured, however, they neither perform a sorting function—allocation of individuals to their best use—nor provide incentives to employees to exert the effort consonant with the higher salary that goes with the higher position. This is because the pay structure in public sector banks is compressed due to the nature of the wage setting process where unions bargain to minimize the distance between their earnings and that set by the government for the Chairman and Managing Director. Also, work culture gets adversely affected as those who do not have the opportunity to be offered a higher level job put in lesser effort and even collude to shirk. Deregulation and increased competition in such a scenario does not act as a disciplining force for enhancing the efficiency of public sector banks. With the implicit insurance by government of support in times of financial difficulty the public sector banks sensitivity to efficiency has been reduced which has resulted in a growth in establishment costs at the expense of provisioning and expenditures on technological upgradation. It is only when public sector banks perceive that the government will not be underwriting their decisions and that they face a hard budget constraint, will they have an incentive to tackle the problem of establishment costs and be able to upgrade technologies, provide better quality services, and become more efficient. The motivation for employees in an efficiently run organization cannot be solely based on rewards such as power and prestige as these are not linked to the performance of an organization. The challenge for public sector banks accordingly is to upgrade technology, downsize, shift the composition of the employees towards officers, introduce multitasking, and a stronger link between pay and performance.

NOTES

1. With the merger of the New Bank of India with Punjab National Bank in 1993 there are now 19 nationalized banks.
2. The regional rural banks and cooperative banks comprise the remaining part of the banking sector which we are not reporting on here.

3. Net Profit = Net Interest Income + Net Non-interest Income – Operating Expenses – Provisions. Working Funds = Total Assets – Contra items (Bills for collection).
4. The Net Profit as a percentage of Working Funds was 0.91 per cent for the decade for private and foreign banks combined and for the latter half of the decade it went up by 9.4 per cent to 1 per cent.
5. The periodization has been decided on the basis of two events. First, the introduction of the new norms of asset classification and income recognition resulted in the public sector banks as a group reporting a net loss in 1992-3 and 1993-4. As this is a response to new regulatory requirements and not the direct result of operational outcomes in those years, including those years in the interpretation of the data will introduce a bias. Second, new private banks were established and entered the market after April 1994 and performance results for these became available from 1995-6. On the basis of these two factors 1995-6 suggested a convenient reference point on which to segment the data for the decade.
6. Following in the steps of the SBI, three other banks—Indian Overseas Bank, Bank of Baroda, and Vysya Bank—entered into agreements with their unions.
7. The introduction of computers has reduced the workload in banks as tasks such as the daily balancing of books which used to take hours now takes minutes. On an average employees in computerized branches finish work two-and-half hours earlier than usual (Mankidy 2000).

REFERENCES

Anand, A., 2000, 'Banking Sector Employment in India: Emerging Trends and Pattern', *Indian Journal of Labour Economics*, 43(4), pp. 1001-12.

Baker, G.P., M.C. Jensen and K.J. Murphy, 1988, 'Compensation and Incentives: Practice Versus Theory', *Journal of Finance*, 43(3), July, pp. 593-616.

Bery, S.K., 1994, 'India: Commercial Bank Reform', in Shakil Faruqui (ed.), *Financial Sector Reforms, Economic Growth, and Stability. Experiences in Selected Asian and Latin American Countries*, The World Bank, Economic Development Institute.

D'Souza, E., 2000, 'The Relationship between Capital Markets and Human Resource Policies: Some Consequences of Flexibility', Twelfth IFCI Annual Lecture, Department of Economics, University of Mumbai, mimeo.

———, 2001, 'Prudential Regulation in Indian Banking', in S. Arumugam (ed.), *Indian Capital Markets—Modern Perspectives and Empirical Evidence*, Allied Publishers Ltd., Mumbai.

Doeringer, P.B. and M.J. Piore, 1971, *Internal Labour Markets and Manpower Analysis,* D.C. Health, Lexington, Mass.

IBA, 1999, 'Database on Indian Banking 1987-98', Economics Department, Indian Banks' Association, Mumbai, December.

———, 2000, 'Indian Banking Year Book, 1999', Indian Banks' Association, Mumbai.

———, 2001, 'Performance Highlights of Banks 1999-2000', Economics Department, Indian Banks' Association, Mumbai, February.

Joshi, V. and I.M.D. Little, 1997, *India's Economic Reforms 1991-2001*, Oxford University Press, New Delhi.

Lazear, E.P. and S. Rosen, 1981, 'Rank-Order Tournaments as Optimum Labour Contracts', *Journal of Political Economy,* October, 89, pp. 841-64.

Mankidy, J., 2000, 'Human Resource Management in Banks: Need for a Paradigm Shift', *Prajnan*, vol. XXVIII, no. 4, pp. 357-72.

Patil, R.H., 1996, 'Contemporary Banking: Competition and Markets', Speech at 17th Bank Economists' Conference, in N. Jadhav (ed.), *Challenges to Indian Banking, Competition, Globalization, and Financial Markets*, Macmillan, New Delhi.

Pillai, R.V., 1974, 'Report of the Committee for Standardization of Pay Scales, Allowances and Perquisites of Officers in the Nationalized Banks with Modifications', Government of India, New Delhi.

RBI, 1999, *Trends and Progress of Banking in India, 1998-99*, RBI, Mumbai.

Sen, K. and R.R. Vaidya, 1997, *The Process of Financial Liberalization in India*, Oxford University Press, New Delhi.

Varkkey, B. and A. Mankidy, 1995, *Human Resources Management in Banking Industry: A Historical Perspective*, National Institute of Bank Management, March, Pune.

Verma, M.S., 1999, 'Report of the Working Group on Restructuring Weak Public Sector Banks', RBI, Mumbai.

Social Costs of Reforms: A Study of Job Loss with Special Reference to Declining Industries in 1990-1998

TIRTHANKAR ROY[1]

Any economic reform process carries with it 'social costs' as well as 'social gains', strictly, gains and costs that cannot be captured in conventional growth accounting. The costs arise primarily because of the accumulation of uncompetitive resources prior to the reform process, the cost of which was earlier borne by consumers and taxpayers. As the reform process unfolds, these resources suffer attrition even as the consumers gain. The term 'social cost' can be, and has been in the context of the Asian crisis in particular,[2] used in a broad sense, to include not only the attrition of labour and capital, but also the uncompensated and unestimated hardships that fall on families or the political upheavals that result from unemployment. This essay is an investigation into a particular aspect of the social costs of the Indian economic reforms in the 1990s, namely, loss of jobs for industrial workers with special reference to declining industries. I prefer the term 'job-loss' to 'unemployment' because the former is a less loaded term. In particular, it includes the possibility of a re-allocation of labour elsewhere, which is in fact a major theme of this paper.

Two changes in the 1990s have adversely affected workers in the organized manufacturing sector. First, directly due to the reforms, many firms have closed down or been forced to reduce the number of workers. There has thus been job-loss directly due to the reforms. Secondly, there has been a subtle but decisive change in the politics of labour. While formally employment practices in the organized sector continue to be bound by rigid laws, many firms have shed labour via voluntary retirement, a course that would have invited a great deal of resistance from trade unions a decade ago. Large and profitable firms have universally reduced their core permanently employed (unionized) labour force. The work formerly done by the core workforce is now being done either by other firms (outsourcing) or by contract labour. In some cases, outsourcing and contract labour are identical. The unionized component of workforce has thus fallen, along with changes in the nature of the unions themselves. In different contexts, this process of disempowerment of labour has been called 'casualization', 'informalization', 'feminization' when there is a gender aspect involved, and decline of trade unionism.

This second process—disempowerment—has not been directly a result of the reforms. But in an indirect way it has been a result of the reforms. It has partly derived from modernization enabled by the reforms, which is one major imperative for restructuring, and partly from a *reformist mentality* ushered in by the policy changes and their quite dramatic effects in the early-1990s. In the past (the early-1980s for example) there was no serious questioning of the labour laws, trade unions tended to be seen as 'weapons of the weak' rather than as powerful 'distributional coalitions', and the implementation of labour laws involved a broadly shared concern for job security.[3] In the 1990s, that mentality disappeared. Labour laws are now seen as a problem by almost anyone other than the central trade unions themselves. The press takes a generally reformist stand. The government as well as the judiciary have followed a broadly non-interventionist role in respect of job-loss and enterprise restructuring in the nineties. And organized labour is more easily seen as groups fighting for sectional interests at the cost of national interest.

What does this change mean for the workers? Optimistically, this whole turmoil can be seen as a massive reallocation of labour and capital to their more productive uses, so that in the aggregate there is an expansion in both employment and investment. There is now sufficient evidence that the first four years after the reforms did see a transition that answers closely to this description. This period recorded unprecedented employment growth. In short, while the *standard* of jobs fell, their *number* increased, and the two processes can be seen as causally related. Because the standard became flexible (thanks to new politics and new mentality), employers could hire more easily (in new profitable avenues opened by the reforms). Reallocation can occur at many levels. Within the firm it occurs via renegotiation of wages, changes in technology, or redeployment of labour. It can also occur between firms, or between the organized sector and the unorganized sector.

The reallocation, however, can be slow due to institutional rigidities that act as barriers to such reallocation. The reallocation can also be painful due to these rigidities. For example, there is a sound case that the legal difficulties of formal exit have encouraged unofficial closure that always involves deprivation for the workers. Reallocation can be painful also because of the absence of adequate safety nets, or in the presence of great inter-sectoral inequalities in labour laws and welfare measures. In that case, generally the reallocation involves lower standards of living, or unemployment that remains uncompensated at the individual level. There is evidence to suggest that these adverse effects did follow in the first half of the 1990s, and joined by the recession, they compounded in the second half of the 1990s.

The essay is an investigation into the most serious of these adverse effects: job-loss. Loss of jobs can occur due to closure or obsolescence as well as to modernization or restructuring in healthy industries. The macroeconomic issues are quite different between these two cases, even though the effects can be identical on the individual worker. The aggregate data on job-loss used in this essay, however, cannot differentiate between these two causes of job-loss. The policy issues concerning safety nets are also more or less identical for the two types, except that issues concerning exit apply only to job-loss due to obsolescence. Inevitably, therefore, these two types of problem overlap in discussions on the effects of the reforms on labour.

The essay asks four specific questions:

- How large have the social costs been for labour engaged in declining industries?
- How far has reallocation of labour from declining to profitable sectors happened?
- What role have labour market institutions played in this transition?
- What lies ahead in terms of structural change and policy option?

The essay is divided into four parts. Since the focus here is on 'declining industries', the first section defines that term more closely. The second section talks about the major macroeconomic issues: estimating job-loss, reallocation, and key policy issues such as formal labour market rigidity but informal labour market flexibility. The third section carries out a study of three declining industries. The fourth presents a summary and policy conclusions.

DEFINITION OF DECLINING INDUSTRIES

Overall, the post-reform period has not seen a general decline in employment or output. To the contrary, it has seen exceptionally good employment growth rates in the organized sector in the first half of the 1990s. There are, however, five specific senses in which decline did occur, with quite severe costs to labour. These relate to the following dimensions: time, industry, firm, sector, and region.

Time-specific Decline

Although the first half of the 1990s saw exceptional growth in the organized sector, the second half saw one of the worst recessions in post-Independence history. The recession was a general phenomenon, and affected almost every sector, either directly, or indirectory via inter-industry linkages and multipliers. The exact causes of the recession have not been adequately researched. It seems that several adverse political and economic factors coincided. Of the economic factors, the impact of the Asian crisis was obviously important. In the first five years of the reforms, large parts of the manufacturing sector, especially textiles, had become exporters of intermediate goods to Asia. Another factor might have been over-expansion of capacity in some industries in the early-1990s. The powerloom textile industry, for example, expanded at a furious pace in the early-1990s driven by very positive market expectations especially in the garment sector. At 2001, more than a third of the looms were reportedly redundant. In both these senses, the late-1990s recession was an effect of India's globalization in the early-1990s. For this essay, the effect of the recession on labour is an important theme, but information on this topic is still very inadequate.

Industry-specific Decline

A few two- and three-digit industry groups have stagnated/declined in employment and profitability throughout the nineties. The most important of these are, cotton spinning and weaving in mills, jute spinning and weaving in mills, and synthetic textiles (Table 1). A few groups within engineering have declined too, chiefly ferrous metals. But in almost all non-textile major groups, the first half of the 1990s was generally profitable. Equally, in all cases, the 1998-9 and 1999-00 were very bad years (Table 2). A subset fell into recession rather early, from 1996. In their case, the reforms may have been directly responsible for their performance, but the effect took a little time. Steel is an example of a reform-related crisis that started biting from the mid-1990s. The current listing of Board for Industrial and Financial Restructuring (BIFR) cases (Tables 3 and 4) show the effect of the recession more clearly. Textiles and metals lead in sickness. Within machinery and metallurgy, there is a big presence of the public sector. In short, the industry picture shows a mix of pre-reform sickness and post-reform sickness. However, in any snapshot, the pre-reform component dominates.

TABLE 1. TWO-DIGIT GROUPS WITH THE LOWEST EMPLOYMENT GROWTH RATES, 1990-7

(%)

	Trend growth rate: 1990-7
All Industries: Organized sector (excluding electricity and gas)	2.1*
Non-metallic mineral products (32)	0.4
Cotton textiles (23)	1.0
Cotton spinning, weaving in mills (235)	-0.5
Basic metals (33)	1.5
Machinery (35, 36)	1.7
Jute textiles (25)	1.9
Jute spinning and weaving (254)	1.5
Minerals: *Refractory and structural clay products + glass (320-1)*	-1.0
Basic metals (33)	0.7*
Iron and steel (330)	-0.4
Fabricated metal products (340)	0.1
Casting (337)	1.4
Machinery: *Industrial machinery (353-4)*	0.6
Transport equipment: *Wagons (372)*	-1.0

NOTES: Numbers in brackets are the NIC codes, the NIC has now been replaced by the International Standard Industrial Classification.

* 1990-8.

SOURCE: Central Statistical Organization (CSO), *Annual Survey of Industries (ASI)*, various years.

TABLE 2. PROFIT-AFTER-TAX AS PERCENTAGE OF GROSS SALES, 1993-2000 (AVERAGE ANNUAL)

	1993-7	*1996-00*
Group A: In recession throughout		
Cotton textiles	-0.7	-5.8
Synthetic textiles	-0.2	-6.8
Jute products	-5.6	-15.2
Rubber and rubber products	-1.9	-5.5
Communication equipment	-2.3	-2.2
Other transport equipment	-1.7	-0.1
Bicycles	-1.2	-0.4
Group B: Early into recession		
Dyes	3.8	-4.4
Cement	3.0	-2.2
Ferrous metals	2.4	-4.0
Textile machinery	3.4	-1.7
Electrical machinery	2.8	-0.8
Manufacturing	3.2	1.4

NOTES: Group A: Industry groups that experienced negative profits throughout the 1990s.
Group B: Industry groups that began to experience negative profits from the mid-1990s.
With a few exceptions, such as software or gems and jewellery, all other major groups saw positive profits in the first period, and negative profits in 1998-9 and 1999-00.

SOURCE: Centre for Monitoring Indian Economy, *Industry: Financial Aggregates and Ratios*, Mumbai, 2001.

TABLE 3. REGISTERED CASES WITH THE BIFR, AS ON 31.12.2000

	Number	*Accumulated losses (Rs. billion)*	*Workers involved*
Textiles	526	91	5,12,591
Metallurgical	485	62	1,52,814
Jute	53	9	1,49,924
Paper and Pulp	197	14	55,834
Electrical machinery	149	29	43,139
Chemicals	202	31	39,030
Sugar	44	9	32,645
All	3,296	551	18,84,565
% of workers in selected industries in all BIFR cases	–	–	52
Approximate % of BIFR workers in organized industry	–	–	20

SOURCE: BIFR website.

TABLE 4. STATEWISE DETAILS OF BIFR CASES, AS ON 31.12.2000

	Number	*Accumulated losses (Rs. billion)*	*Workers*
West Bengal	271	95	5,55,178
Maharashtra	593	96	2,18,837
Andhra Pradesh	356	40	1,85,727
Gujarat	287	51	1,73,025
Bihar	67	41	1,67,933
Uttar Pradesh	293	49	1,50,176
Tamil Nadu	301	35	99,934

SOURCE: BIFR website.

Firm-level Decline

In cotton textiles, jute textiles and synthetic textiles, the reforms rendered many firms uncompetitive. But it also offered a few firms that were better managed, more creditworthy, and already technologically advanced, the chance to globalize with great success. In industry case-studies further on, we shall see that the reforms, thus, had the effect mainly of a sharp polarization even within the so-called declining sectors.

Sectoral Decline

In overall scale, neither the organized sector nor the unorganized sector shows any declining trend over the 1990s. The organized sector trend has been generally rising, and the unorganized sector fluctuating. But these fluctuations may result from the quality of the surveys. If there were real fluctuations, a relationship can be suggested between the organized and the unorganized sector trends, as we shall see.

Regional Dimension

Since declining industries and firms have a bias towards older sectors and their problems have pre-reform roots, labour affected remains concentrated in the older industrialized regions.

To sum up, there was no net decline in employment or profitability during the 1990s. The reform process offered opportunities as well as created competition. The net effect was, in fact, a large growth in jobs. The problems of firm-bankruptcy and loss of jobs have been especially acute in (a) certain industries where these problems have had older roots, (b) certain firms within these industries, (c) the late-1990s recession, and (d) the older industrialized states.

MACRO ISSUES CONCERNING LABOUR

In the literature on post-reform labour two macroeconomic issues appear frequently, these are:

(1) reallocation between organized and unorganized sector, and
(2) changes in labour market institutions as a result of or causing decline.

In addition, three more macroeconomic issues, not so widely discussed as yet, require some attention. These are:

(1) measurement of redundancy,
(2) measurement of job-loss, and
(3) effects of the recession.

These five issues are taken up in this section for detailed discussion. These appear in a somewhat different sequence, beginning with measurement.

Measuring Redundancy

There are several estimates of levels of redundancy in the organized sector for the early 1990s.[4] The most recent such estimate put the number of redundant workers in industry in 1990-1 at 1.4 million, 0.4 million in the Central Public Sector Undertakings, and one million in the private organized sector.[5] These figures represented 18 and 13 per cent of the employment in the two sectors. However, these figures include a large percentage of workers employed in already sick industries. Excluding them, approximately half a million workers in the organized sector could be seen as under threat of losing jobs when the reforms unfolded. Surprisingly, calculations below suggest that the actual extent of job loss in manufacturing has been about a quarter of a million or close to this figure.

Measuring Job-loss in the 1990s

Aggregate change in employment during a period is by definition a sum of jobs created and jobs lost. Jobs lost, if we can measure it, should give us a gross measure of the hardship for labour during the 1990s.

There is no direct data on jobs created and jobs lost in the organized sector. Based on the data supplied in one table in the Annual Survey of Industries or ASI (Appendix Table 2, Industrial Characteristics by Year of Production), an approximate measure can be created. This is derived in the following way. The table shows how many factories (and employment, output, etc., therein) reported having started operation during, say, 1980-90. Let us call the incremental employment G, representing new jobs created during 1980-90. G should equal G1+G2, where G1 is new jobs in firms started during the period, and G2 is new jobs in firms that expanded during the period. The G1 figures change according to when the survey is done. The number of firms who report in 1990 as having started in 1980-90 will be different from the number who report in 1995 as having started between 1980-90 by the extent of exit of some of the 1990 respondents between 1990-5. So, the best measure is one recorded immediately after the period of interest. Let us call employment in 1990 N2 and employment in 1980 N1. Then, L or jobs lost during 1980s is by definition:

$$L = N1 + (G1+G2) - N2$$

This being an identity it does not explain anything, but *ex post*, when we already have figures for N1 and N2, it can be used to decompose net change in jobs into gains and losses.

Several cautions are necessary in applying this formula. L, being derived as a residual, includes persons who retired or quit voluntarily, and not only those who lost jobs against their wishes. However, it is a fair assumption that retirement is a constant proportion of the workforce over time, balanced exactly by new recruitment, and therefore does not explain changes in L between periods. It is also fair to assume that those who quit jobs were re-employed relatively quickly so that that should not influence L either when measured over a long enough period.

A more serious problem is that the dataset does not capture jobs created due to expansion in running firms, or G2. The ASI table gives measures of G1. It does not give measures of G2.[6] There are two alternatives. First, since the number of factories lost can be more simply measured by (where the superscript * refers to factories)

$$L^* = N1^* + G1^* - N2^*$$

we can assume that the factories exited had the same average employment size as that of the factories started. That is, we can assume that

$$L/L^* = G1/G1^* \text{ or } L = G1/G1^*.L^*$$

This gives us a proxy measure for gross job-loss, via factories. Second, assuming G1 and G2 are always positive, we can use only G1 figure, with the knowledge that it gives us the lowest benchmark of job-loss. In Table 5, we use only the second alternative. The assumption that G2 is zero or very low is not so very odd after all, for in reality there are very few old firms in the organized sector that created a significant number of new jobs. The drive to shed jobs was overwhelming and universal among the old firms. So, the low benchmark of job-loss should not be very different from reality.

There is another caution. When long periods are taken for comparison, the data on factories started will not record factories that were started and closed within that period. There is, however, no reason to assume that a large number should be affected by such short life, or that the short-life problem changes over time. Subject to these cautions and limitations, what do the data show?

TABLE 5. JOBS GAINED AND LOST IN THE ORGANIZED SECTOR, 1980-98

	1980-90	*1990-7*	*1997-8 and 1998-9*
1. Factories started (no.)	49,448	40,261	0[1]
2. Employment in factories started (m)	2.18	1.92	0[1]
3. Factories exited (no.)	30,570	17,879	569
4. Employment in factories exited (m)[2]	2.14	0.45	0.29
5. 3 as % of factories in initial year	33.6	16.3	0.5
6. 4 as % of employment in initial year	29.1	6.1	3.9
7. Worker per factory started (no.)	44	48	–
8. Worker per factory exited (no.)	70	25	505[3]

NOTES: [1]By assumption. [2]Calculated by using the formula L = N1 + (G1 + G2) – N2 (see text). On the assumption that G1 and G2 are both positive, given that G2 is not available, the estimated L should be seen as the minimum gross job-loss. 3. Influenced by a few large closures and the small number of observations.

SOURCE: CSO, *ASI, Summary Results for the Factory Sector*, 1990-1, 1997-8, 1998-9.

Table 5 makes a comparison between three periods: 1980-90, 1990-7, and 1997-9, the last captures the impact of the recession. The table suggests four conclusions.

1. The extent of gross job-loss in the 1990s was relatively small, if the recession is ignored. This estimate of gross jobs lost closely tallies with ILO estimates of redundancy in the organized sector industry. Out of total redundancy estimated for 1990 (1.4 million), if we exclude the figure for jobs in firms that were already sick in 1990, the potential redundancy figure comes to about 0.6 million. Our estimate of gross jobs lost is 0.7 million.
2. For 1998-9, we do not have estimate for G, because the full published ASI volume is not yet available. However, if we assume G to be zero, we get a measure of job-loss that is quite large for one year. This is the lower bound of the estimate of gross jobs lost in 1998-9, it will become larger if G is positive.
3. Table 5 also suggests that the recession hit the larger-sized firms particularly hard. Press reports do suggest that this may be so. 'In the past two years [1995-7] there has been a distinct change in the kind of companies knocking at BIFRs doors. Some of the bigger private sector companies have declared themselves sick and gone to the BIFR.'[7] However, the reasons for a change in scale are not clear yet.
4. The fourth conclusion from the table relates to comparison between the 1980s and the 1990s. It is by now clear that the 1990s, by contrast with the 1980s, did not see a large rise in output or income growth, but did see a significant increase in gross jobs created, growth rate of employment, and the output-elasticity of employment in the organized sector (Tables 5 and 6). The other major difference is that the rate of growth of average real wages slowed down greatly in the 1990s. Given almost identical growth rates in real value-added per worker, this would mean acceleration in profit per worker in real terms. There is no question that slowdown in wages contributed to increased profitability.

What did this slowdown in wages mean? Was there a real labour market change involved? Did it make employers willing to hire more liberally? First of all, there may not have been a slowdown in

TABLE 6. RELATIONSHIP BETWEEN WAGE, EMPLOYMENT AND OUTPUT IN THE ORGANIZED SECTOR: 1980-90 AND 1992-7

	1980-90	*1992-7*
Average growth rate in		
Output	8.07	9.00
Employment	0.06	3.02
Real wage	6.07	3.05
Output-elasticity of employment	0.04	0.31

individual wage rates, but a change in the composition of work-force towards lesser permanent employees and more casual employees. That such a change occurred in the 1990s is beyond question. It is also indisputable that labour market flexibility increased (with consequent wage flexibility) in the 1990s due to changes in labour market institutions (more on this below).

The 1980s, indeed, has been the subject of a lively debate in recent times. In organized manufacturing, the 1980s saw rapid increase in real wages, moderate increase in productivity, but almost no change in employment. These features have been named the syndrome of 'jobless growth'. Needless to say, one theory, perhaps the mainstream theory, for jobless growth holds labour militancy as the independent variable. However, dissenting views exist, which look at the nature of technological change in the 1980s.[8]

Why did jobless growth turn into job-friendly growth in the early-1990s? One answer is that industrial composition changed in favour of labour-intensive sectors. Most exportable sectors are, in fact, labour-intensive. This answer lays more stress on the demand effects of the reform. A second answer focuses on the dynamics of the labour market. That is, on the supply side, and suggests that the employment growth resulted from a coincidence of reforms with changes in industrial relations. Incidence of labour militancy came down quite significantly in the 1900s (see Table 7), and may have encouraged more recruitment while slowing down wage growth. By contrast, employment was sluggish in the 1980s because of labour militancy, often state-backed.

The analysis in Table 5, however, reveals an important feature of the decade, 1980-90, that has been more or less ignored in the 'jobless growth' debate. The apparent slow growth rate in employment in the decade does not mean that jobs grew more slowly then than in the following decade. It actually conceals the fact that *jobs were lost on*

TABLE 7. WORKERS INVOLVED (MILLIONS) IN INDUSTRIAL DISPUTES, 1986-97

	1986-91	*1992-7*
India		
Strikes	7.1	4.0
Lockouts	1.6	2.0
Andhra Pradesh		
Strikes	2.2	0.6
Lockouts	0.6	1.2
West Bengal		
Strikes	0.5	0.3
Lockouts	1.3	1.4
Maharashtra		
Strikes	0.4	0.0
Lockouts	0.1	0.2
Tamil Nadu		
Strikes	0.8	0.1
Lockouts	0.1	0.1

SOURCE: R. Dutt, 'Regional Pattern of Industrial Relations in India', *Indian Journal of Labour Economics*, 42(4), 2000.

an exceptionally large scale in the 1980s, to the extent of almost a quarter of the employment level in 1980. These jobs were lost in older industries. Jobless growth was influenced by *large closures*, the most famous examples of which occurred in textiles and engineering. In the period 1991-6, such large-scale closures were rare, closures occurred more at the firm level, and total job-loss was very little, about 2 per cent of 1991 employment.

Between the 1980s and the 1990s, there was a shift from industry-wide closures to firm-specific closures. This change suggests that in respect of labour, the main difference between the 1980s and the 1990s was not one of 'more' or 'less' militancy, but of change in bargaining institutions. Industry-wide unions were in decline all through the 1980s, making way for firm- specific bargaining. Closures, to the extent they can be attributed to labour factors like militancy or wage-rigidity, also ceased to be industry-wide in the 1990s.

Reallocation between Organized and Unorganized Sectors

The reallocation issue is centrally related to the expectation that the reforms will reduce employment in the organized sector, as we shall see.

The organized sector is defined as factories covered by the Factories Act. The unorganized sector consists of production units not covered by the Act. The distinction is crucial in explanations of employment trends, because regulation and politics matter to hiring and firing of labour. It matters most obviously via labour militancy and wage-rigidity. Until recently, the data to measure net employment effects of the reforms on the unorganized sector were not available. Employment in factories is available annually. But no up-to-date estimate of unorganized sector employment was available. Recent National Sample Survey (NSS) studies of the 55th round redress that gap greatly and enable a general answer to the question above. This dataset consists of two NSS surveys of unorganized manufacturing in 1989 and 1994, and employment surveys for 1993-4 and 1999-00. We also have Economic Census estimates for industrial employment, but the census and the NSS estimates differ widely, mainly due to differences in the underlying work participation rates for women. On balance, scholarly opinion favours the use of NSS.

Employment in the unorganized sector fell marginally in the period 1989-94. This was, in fact, an average over rapid growth in exportable sectors like garments and leather products, and fall in old-style utilitarian handicrafts like handlooms and pottery. Interestingly, within the unorganized sector too, there was stagnation in real wages and growth in productivity, which suggests that politics of organized labour alone cannot account for the wage-productivity trend in the organized sector. By contrast with the early 1990s, in the late 1990s, unorganized sector employment seems to have grown substantially (Table 8).

There is no clear evidence in Table 8 to suggest that the trends in the two sectors are interrelated. That conclusion, however, may result from over-aggregation in both sectors. Both figures are net of gains and losses within the respective sector. Since we do have figures for

TABLE 8. EMPLOYMENT IN MANUFACTURING

(millions)

	1989	*1994*	*1999*
Unorganized	35.0	33.4	35.1
Organized (excluding electricity and gas)	8.2	8.2	8.6
Total	43.2	41.6	43.7

SOURCES: National Sample Survey Organisation, 45th, 51st and 55th Rounds, CSO, *ASI*.

gross jobs lost in the organized sector, let us use that data to see if a different conclusion can be suggested. A combination of Tables 6 and 8 does hint at a reallocation. As we see from Table 6, in the first half of the 1990s, there was no net loss of employment in the organized sector. Gross job-loss was small and gross job gained was large. It is certainly plausible that some of those who lost jobs went into the unorganized sector (well-documented for the cotton textile industry, see below) whereas some who gained jobs were recruited from potential entrants into the unorganized sector, in the net leading to a fall in the employment in the latter. In the later part of the decade, however, the impact of the recession may have pushed large numbers from the organized to the unorganized sector. Interestingly, productivity has continued to grow in the unorganized sector during 1993-8, which suggests that the sector could employ at least some of the excess supply productively.

In theory the two trends should be interrelated. The basic theory about the employment effects of reforms assumes two divisions in the labour force: one along organizational lines and the other along import competition. If it is the case that the sector where labour tends to be more organized (that is wages are protected) is also the import-substituting sector, then the effect of tariff reforms will be to render workers unemployed in that sector.[9] Had it produced non-tradeable, labour would not be affected by imports. If it had market-driven wages, wages could be driven down for adjustment. But if import-substitution, wage-protection, and wage-rigidity combine, employment will fall.

Unemployed workers will crowd into the unorganized sector, whether into mainly manufacturing, agriculture, or the services depends on where import-substitution was effective within the unorganized sector. Generally, segments of unorganized manufacturing can decline too, but by and large the unorganized sector does not face too much competition because (a) it produces non-tradeable, and (b) in the Indian context, it utilizes the abundant input, labour.

Earlier work has shown reallocation to have taken place from organized manufacturing to non-manufacturing in the first two years of the reforms.[10] Our data—which deal with the whole of the 1990s and only with manufacturing—suggest reallocation of labour between sectors *within manufacturing* (Tables 6 and 8 read together, see text above).

The prediction that organized sector employment must fall due to greater competition is, however, simplistic and may get complicated by several factors. First, access to technology after the reforms may have a positive effect on organized sector. Total employment may increase even if employment elasticity falls.[11] Second, if wage rigidity was a problem before, more competition can bring down wage-rigidity and have a positive effect on employment. Third, the gender composition of the workforce may change in both the organized sector and the unorganized sector. Organized sector workers are mainly males. Clearly, more males than females are likely to lose jobs. These males then crowd into the unorganized sector. What happens then? There are sectors such as clothing where there is a positive preference for females. There are also sectors such as tanning or metal-work where there is a positive preference for males. In such sectors, nothing should change. In sectors where males and females are substitutable, a competition and displacement between males and females may take place. But what these sectors are we do not know yet, it is an important issue for further research. The net gender effect of organized sector job-loss is likely to be fourfold,

(a) rise in male unemployment or underemployment,
(b) rise in female employment, and
(c) increasing casualization or informalization of work since permanency is rare in the unorganized sector and among females.[12]
(d) Shifts in industrial organization, for women seem to prefer different organizational set-ups than a factory. Non-factory forms of work-place may increasingly appear, even though the family firm may be on decline. Again, this issue of the gendered work-place requires more study. One common form in the new scenario seems to be home-based subcontracting, which involves paid workers working from their homes.

Fourthly, job-loss in the organized sector is likely to be intensive in unskilled labour.

Institutions

Institutional issues come to the forefront of any discussion of the declining industries for two reasons. In the case of shifts of workers into the unorganized sector, the quality of jobs changes drastically. It changes in respect of wages, security, severance commitment, 'casualization', etc. In the unorganized sector, there is either no legal regime at all, or the regime is provided by the Contract Labour Act, which has many loopholes in theory or in practice. Second, large declining firms share some common institutional features that are relevant to labour, mainly various forms of rigidity applicable to exit and employment. Two forms of rigidity are discussed most frequently, and both have become major issues of debate and political confrontation. These are, exit policy and lay-off. In an informal way, labour market institutions in the 1990s have changed towards greater flexibility. Many firms and industries have quietly bypassed these formal rigidities. But the very informality that takes such processes outside large-scale bargaining can also deprive workers of their dues. Such deprivations have been glaring in the case of unofficial closures.

Exit rigidity: Exit rigidity means procedures making closure difficult. The present legal regime governing exit was erected in 1985 when the Sick Industries and Companies Act (SICA) was introduced. The SICA originated in a report submitted in 1981 that pointed out the need for special legislation to deal with industrial sickness (perpetual bankruptcy). Before that, several committees had been set up, but none had led to sweeping institutional changes. The SICA made it mandatory for firms with employment of 50 or more to refer to the quasi-judicial body BIFR (started in 1987) before closure. Public sector undertakings were brought under the BIFR in 1991. The underlying presumptions were that firms generally became sick due to management failure, and firms could always be revived under different management. The motivation was to prevent jobs and assets from destruction.

It is now evident that the premises, the motives, and the procedures employed by the SICA regime were unsound. Firms can become sick due to a variety of demand and supply factors, management failure is just one of them. When the reason is exogenous and not within the firm's control, rehabilitation is pointless. Exit rigidity may keep one firm alive, but hurts both labour and capital at the macro level. The freedom of resource allocation and redeployment of factors of production is fundamental to any enterprise, and in modern views, even a defining feature of entrepreneurship. Barriers to resource reallocation may scare away new investment when investment risks increase generally, and may lead to *de facto* closure such as lockouts, which is costly to both the employees and the employers.

As for BIFR, it almost always faces an impossible task of coordination and management. The referral process typically takes several years. Its definition of 'sickness' is too restrictive and cannot prevent it, but catches firms when they are beyond rehabilitation.[13] A report on industrial sickness also pointed out how Reserve Bank of India guidelines on supply of cheap funds to sick firms have been misused, leading to accumulation of bad debts.[14] If the BIFR decides on closure, the process can take years of adjudication during which workers must wait for their dues. There are reports of workers committing suicides in the course of this waiting.

A sick company, sick under the definition of the SICA, can appeal to the BIFR, which gives it a hearing, institutes an inquiry if necessary, and appoints an Operating Agency (OA), typically the largest creditor, to prepare a rehabilitation package. In the BIFRs own admission, the OA is expectedly biased about the kind of revival package it wants to institute.[15] By a Supreme Court judgement, the company gets legal immunity from its creditors once it is under the BIFR fold. In further hearing, the rehabilitation package is accepted, rejected, or modified. The number of referrals ran into close to a hundred until 1997, and to several hundreds annually thereafter. The disposal rate is much smaller. BIFR decisions can be appealed against at an appellate authority. All this adds to the time taken for a company to approach the stage of closure. Only after rehabilitation fails can a company approach closure, which is then handled by the courts.

Finally, there are reports of misuse. The provision of legal immunity seems to have had an 'adverse selection' effect. In 1998, a number of referrals allegedly came from companies that were not necessarily 'sick', but whose directors were liable under the Negotiable Instruments Act for writing cheques that bounced. The provision of legal immunity and the high costs of market borrowings apparently drove a number of companies to BIFR in 1998.[16]

This regime may now be replaced by a National Company Law Tribunal, which will be in charge of rehabilitation, closure, and other insolvency issues dealt with the Company Law Board. However, the essential nature of the system is not likely to change, for any closure will still be mandatorily preceded by a rehabilitation attempt.

Formal labour-market rigidity: Classical wage-rigidity is far less an issue in the 1990s, whether due to political or economic changes. However, other forms of rigidity continue. The most important of these concerns layoff and redeployment. The Industrial Disputes Act lays down rules governing layoff, retrenchment and compensation. In sum, the rules make it mandatory for a firm to seek government permission to lay off any regular employee, to pay compensation, and to serve adequate notice (*de facto* seek the union's permission) for redeploying any worker.[17] In case of dismissal, the order can be contested in a petition to the government and lead to a lengthy negotiation. In practice, retrenchment is difficult except in cases of proven criminal acts. In short, the rules are stringent, and their practice, at the courts or at the political level, has been loaded in favour of labour until the recent past.

The cost of retrenchment is only one of the problems, the one more easily handled. To increase labour market flexibility and yet reduce the social costs of flexibility, the government announced the start of National Renewal Fund (NRF) in 1992-3. The Fund was to support retrenchment, retraining, redeployment, and compensation due to closure. For the unorganized sector, the NRF was also meant to finance employment generation schemes. The experience of the NRF in the period 1993-8 showed that:

(a) Rs. 18 billion was spent on various schemes, 89 per cent consisted of Voluntary Retirement Schemes (VRS) packages for about 1,00,000 public sector employees,
(b) the number of persons covered under the NRF steadily fell,
(c) budgetary provisions also fell, and was considered grossly inadequate,
(d) other programes such as counselling, retraining, redeployment involved about 50,000 workers, and
(e) all other schemes such as soft loans for restructuring, employment generation schemes, etc., were more or less ignored.
(f) Further, the ILO found that until 1995, a majority of those under VRS were public sector employees of managerial cadre, which made the compensation unsustainably expensive for the government.[18]

After 1995, the NRF became wholly associated with the divestment process in the central public sector undertakings. Whereas until mid-1998, only about 1,00,000 public sector workers opted for VRS under the NRF, the ILO estimated the total redundancy in the public sector at 3.4 million, and redundancy in the PSUs at 0.4 million. VRS coverage, in other words, was less than 25 per cent of redundancy. In October 2000, the NRF was abolished and replaced with a scheme to supply direct budgetary support to individual ministries according to their VRS requirements. In the private sector, voluntary retirements have been implemented on a wider scale, though the exact magnitudes and costs are uncertain.

The more difficult problems are associated with legal reforms. There is definitely greater political awareness and urgency about reforms in this area. Frequent pronouncements by the concerned Ministers on labour law reform testify to this. These include statements made by the Prime Minister on the May Day, 2001, the deliberations at the Indian Labour Conference, and the Finance Minister's budget statements that referred to job losses and safety nets. A bill has been passed making the registration of new unions subject to more stringent conditions than before. The minimum employee limit for an industrial establishment to come under the Industrial Disputes Act is proposed to be increased from 50 to 1,000, though writing in the third quarter of 2002 it seems unlikely that this measure can actually become a law. Under the Industries (Development and Regulation) Act 1947, employment in the organized sector is subject to 47 central laws relating to hours, security, wages, safety, lay off, etc. The Second Labour Commission is expected to modify and rationalize these laws in several respects. On the other side, the organized trade unions, with 2.2 million members, have vowed to fight the government's 'anti-labour policies'. Large May Day rallies in 2001 testified to that resolve. The key question is, how can labour reforms be carried through without, or with, consent of the central trade unions.

The rigidity-flexibility choice arises in a broader macroeconomic debate that concerns the move desired by policy-makers and resisted by the organized sector labour to shift from an uncompetitive and anti-employment labour regime to a 'low road' of industrialization that involves competitive labour regimes. The existing regime discourages more employment because it guarantees those employed in the organized sector more than their fair share given the capacity of the economy. The 'low road' involves a totally deregulated labour market that can fully exploit the true labour costs in a labour-abundant low-wage economy. By contrast the 'high road' is based on efficiency and innovation rather than low labour costs.[19] However, this issue need not concern us further.

Concern with labour regimes is also heightened by India-China comparison. Before the East Asian crisis, comparisons between India and East Asian policy regimes brought home the glaring differences in their respective labour regimes.[20] After the crisis, it is the spectre of China that is looming large upon India. Relative labour cost is a key issue in the question of how well India can withstand Chinese imports in the more liberal import regime. It is now well-known that despite lower wages in India, competitiveness in labour-intensive manufactures is low because of very low productivity of labour. In turn, higher productivity in China is partly due to the readiness of labour to accept greater shop-floor discipline, responsibility for quality, retrenchments, retraining, and redeployment. All this is more difficult to achieve in an average firm in India due to either past practices or political resistance.

Informally Flexible

The rigidities in the formal labour regime matter crucially to the public sector, but to a minority of firms in the private sector. In the rest of the manufacturing sector, two sets of change—one in the sphere of industrial relations, and the other in the sphere of employment practices—have reinforced one another to enable a number of options about retrenchment, redeployment, and retraining, that did not exist in the 1980s. It is now well known that in the last 10 years or so, industrial relations in private sector industry has changed towards:

- De-unionization
- Retreat of the state from collective bargaining, and consequent weakening of collective bargaining
- Fragmentation of bargaining unit from industry down to factory, plant, division
- Slowdown in strikes.

In the 1990s, major changes have taken place both in modes of employment and in modes of collective bargaining to allow for greater flexibility. The roots of some of these changes are older, and go back to the turbulent 1980s. The most important options are

- contractual employment
- voluntary retirement

- ban on recruitment
- outsourcing.

An implicit ban on recruitment in manufacturing has been followed since the 1980s by a number of large firms. Voluntary retirement schemes have been implemented in almost all the major firms, with minimum or no resistance from labour.[21] A large number of firms have been subcontracting previously integrated processes and services to other firms, in the process shedding permanent workforce.[22] Reduction in the permanent (unionized) component of workforce, or 'off-loading' labour,[23] seems to derive from two desires on the part of the employers. First, the prospect of achieving a smaller and more amenable core workforce. And second, the fear that in non-core work, a unionized permanent labour force is a waste of bargaining energy. Contract employment means subcontracting parts of factory work not usually related to the manufacturing process to other firms (usually labour supply agencies). Typically, such intra-factory services as canteen or maintenance are routinely contracted out. This has become a universal practice in western India. Contract employment not only reduces the possibility of resistance (since contract workers are non-unionized), it also saves the employer money otherwise to be spent on benefits. Subcontracting, however, is not limited to such intra-factory employment. It also includes an ever-increasing practice of acquiring parts and processes from outside. Industries that were formerly not heavy subcontractors such as pharmaceuticals have now become so.

Perhaps the most important institutional change has been the decline of state-backed industry-wide unions, and industry-wide bargaining.[24] Outside the public sector, such unions are considerably weaker now. In the public sector, the de-linking of wage issues from budgetary support in the early-1990s effectively ended industry-wide bargaining on wages. Their increasingly close identification with bankrupt public sector firms has contributed greatly to the political isolation of the central trade unions and weakened their legitimacy in public eye as representatives of labour in general. 'Labour regime' is a term used to characterize labour market institutions, especially, labour's power to influence its own absolute and relative economic situation. In terms of this literature, Indian labour regime is decisively changing. It seems to be changing from a pluralist regime, where unions can play a role in national politics via their dependent relationship with political groups, to a truly decentralized regime where unions have little or no relationship with political groups.[25]

If this is the general picture of the 1990s, declining industries differ from it somewhat. They do employ contract labour heavily to achieve an extra measure of flexibility. On the other hand, industry-wide unions have survived somewhat more in declining industries, and play a more active role. This feature owes partly to the presence of the public sector in some of them (such as the National Textile Corporation in cotton textiles, or National Jute Mills Corporation in jute). Partly it is a result of an internal paralysis, many firms in declining sectors cannot either exit or negotiate with labour a profitable solution. The greater role for industry unions is also partly a matter of history and regional politics. In cotton mills, officially there is still a single representative union of the workers (whose monopoly the workers effectively rejected in the famous 1982-3 strike). In jute textiles, on the other hand, the government of West Bengal and the trade unions have traditionally played an activist and interventionist role.

On the other hand, firms that have survived within the declining industries, aggressively pursue contract employment and plant-level bargaining. For this reason, intra-industry divergence in wages, employment security, permanent-contract proportion, and modes of bargaining, tend to be especially wide in declining industries.

INDUSTRY CASE-STUDIES

Cotton Textiles

The most intensively studied case of decline is the composite cotton textile mills of Mumbai and Ahmedabad. Among the oldest factories in India, these firms started becoming bankrupt from the late-1970s. The 1982-3 textile strike was an opportunity for several of them to close down permanently, which then were nationalized to form part of the National Textile Corporation (NTC). The other mills continued, but not for long. More mills became loss-making in the late-1980s and the early-1990s. The macroeconomic environment was becoming adverse for the majority of the mills from the 1970s itself. On the one hand, the powerloom industry made mill weaving steadily uncompetitive for comparable cloth, due to a variety of cost differences. On the other hand, various restrictions prevented mills from changing technology and producing non-competing products. From 1985, the latter restrictions eased, but by then only a few mills were able to utilize the fruits of a liberalized regime on import of machinery. Land values soared so high in the mid-1990s, that many mills found themselves faced with a choice, either to restructure, or to sell land and close down. Given the risks and costs of the former route, they chose the latter.[26] In all mills, there was greater informal flexibility after the 1982 strike. Indeed, more than a hundred thousand workers are said to have lost their jobs at the time of the strike itself. In the successful mills, the mode of bargaining changed towards greater plant-level negotiations.

The impact of the reforms on the cotton textile industry has not been one-sided. Upon dynamic mills it has been very positive. Access to world market and world technology gave a few mills the opportunity to globalize in very profitable ways (in the 1998 recession nearly all of them fared very badly). Many spinning mills became successful exporters, and new investments soared in spinning and weaving. On the rest of the composite mills, the reforms had had no direct effect, positive or negative. However, closure was probably speeded up, under tacit hands-off policy on behalf of the state.

Between 1985 and 1996, 111 mills, of which 52 were composite spinning-weaving-processing mills, closed down. By a rough estimation, about 2,72,000 persons lost their jobs in this period (Table 9).[27] Of this figure, well over hundred thousand occurred in Mumbai and Gujarat each. There is now a substantial literature on the effects of mill closure on workers.[28] In the rest of this section we present a summary of the main findings of this literature.

TABLE 9. EMPLOYMENT IN THREE INDUSTRIES FACING LABOUR-RELATED PROBLEMS

Years	*Cotton mills*	*Man-made fibre spinning and weaving*	*Jute mills*
1990-1	6,16,015	1,86,043	1,89,856
1991-2	5,89,558	1,72,545	1,92,818
1992-3	5,88,158	1,79,750	1,90,747
1993-4	5,87,208	1,87,383	1,64,658
1994-5	5,78,775	1,90,634	1,75,646
1995-6	6,10,280	2,20,287	2,45,836
1996-7	5,84,241	2,26,668	1,98,359
1997-8	5,73,108	2,06,019	1,99,481

The first signs of closure are irregularity in payment of dues. Almost always, such signs fail to alert the financial institutions, which tend to be less affected than are the private and weak creditors. It is reported that unofficial closures follow a pattern. The private mills simply stop paying electricity bills until electricity connection was cut, when operations ceased. Such *de facto* closure is accompanied with non-payment of workers' dues. The matter ends up in court. If the court decides on a legal closure, the whole process to liquidation may take several years. On the employers' side, assets remain locked up in the mills premises, unless these are quietly removed with the help of the underworld. In the event of unofficial closure, rarely is any compensation paid, or too little is paid. However, experience here varies from mill to mill. In smaller towns, where only one or two mills exist, compensation records tend to be fairer.

A series of studies on the effects of closure on workers reveal certain common conclusions:

- Levels of unemployment due to job-loss vary between surveys. Most surveys find a minority (about a quarter) of workers remaining unemployed even after a year. There is often a long period of initial unemployment, this is partly due to search costs and preferences, workers at first look for old-type factory jobs. The length of the period depends upon the extent of help received from relatives.
- Age is a barrier to re-employment and retraining.
- New employment has the following general characteristics:
  - (a) informalization, or greater extent of participation in the informal sector,
  - (b) departure from permanency, return to job-security being extremely rare,
  - (c) greater extent of self-employment, that is, a general departure from wage-work,
  - (d) on average much reduced levels of earnings, not to speak of welfare provisions.
- Usual new occupations include factory-work (in Ahmedabad), operating small trades and shops, agriculture (in more rural districts), security services, transport, casual labour.
- Compensation is generally of small amount and rarely supplied. When available, it plays almost no role in facilitating re-

employment. More usually it is used for payment of debts, or construction of house. Full legal compensation is rare. VRS exists only in the case of closure of public sector mills.

- Loss of job is a multiple social loss: it is loss of community, credit (the Textile Labour Association of Ahmedabad ran a bank that faced problems as its membership dwindled), dignity and self-respect. For workers in smaller towns like Surat, Navsari or Bilimora, getting a mill job used to mean a major improvement in economic and social welfare—closure is correspondingly a social decline. There is also a family adjustment. Children may give up studies. Marriages may be postponed. Wives need to look for work. The usually very small prior work-participation of adult women in millhand families, in fact, heightens the costs of job-loss, a point missed in the scholarship on the effects of mill closure. In that sense, job-loss and social practices join hands in making it harder for the workers.

An important issue in this literature on closure is the question of the role of the trade unions. Officially, both Mumbai and Ahmedabad have monopoly unions, but the monopoly lost legitimacy and was in practice broken up at least 20 years ago. The few surviving and profitable mills have invariably decentralized bargaining institutions. For the closed and sick mills, the unions have generally played a non-interventionist role in prevention of closure. Their role has been confined to fighting for compensation after the closure happens. However, in Ahmedabad, the steady loss of membership has seriously constrained the main union, the Textile Labour Association. The battle cannot be taken very far by labour simply because the industry is almost bankrupt and public support for mill workers has been more or less eroded in the 1990s. Studies on closure, however, miss these circumstantial changes and find the lack of a strong movement against closure a matter of surprise.[29]

Jute Textiles

There are 73 jute mills in the country, of which 59 are situated in West Bengal. These jute mills employ around 1.94 lakh regular workers. There are many casual workers, the exact number is unknown. One recent figure that puts the number of casual workers at six times the number of regular workers seems grossly exaggerated.[30] As of 1998, six mills were closed, but in the first half of 2001, at least four others joined them. A few specialized mills, such as Champadany, Hooghly, or Ludlow, are very profitable, thanks to greater modernization, better product mix, efficient manpower management and managerial flexibility. A set of profitable mills is 100 per cent export-oriented units. The public sector National Jute Mills Corporation owns six mills of which five are located in West Bengal. It was declared a sick industrial company by the BIFR in 1992, and since then has had to struggle for access to funds. This struggle worsened in the late-1990s with inflation in raw jute prices. Within the private sector, there are great differences. The largest mills tend to be diversified and profitable, and they usually belong to the Indian Jute Mills Association, which is the main negotiating body. However, the majority of the mills do not belong to this association.

In the early-1980s, jute tended to be written off as an industry without future. However, the industry has not declined any further thereafter. The production volume of jute goods has fluctuated widely around an almost constant average of 1.3 million tonnes during the period, 1985-2000. But the composition of jute goods has changed. The main product has all along been material for packaging. Domestically, the demand has been artificially maintained by a government order making it mandatory for some bulk commodity producers to use jute bags. There has been a lot of resistance to this order, and the cement industry has stopped following it totally. Now, however, there is an increasing preference for jute bags because of its eco-friendly qualities. The industry's dependence on protection has also fallen at the same time, as new products made of jute have fared quite well in the market. The export market is growing due to both diversification and environmental awareness. 1995 especially was a kind of turnaround year for jute.

As in cotton textiles, the direct effect of the reforms on jute was encouragement to export and modernization. The outcome was, a set of mills restructured and became fully export oriented in the 1990s. These mills manufacture high quality yarn/twine, jute decorative fabrics, fine hessian cloth, jute bags and blended fabrics. By and large the industry manufactures material for various types of packing bags. At the same time, the majority of the mills continue to function more or less along old lines—traditional products with traditional machinery, high labour cost, low productivity, and fluctuating profits. When under pressure these mills squeeze labour.

As in cotton textiles, the reforms have had an indirect effect, disempowerment of unions. Central trade unions command less and less following in jute. Unions have decentralized and fragmented. Every major incident of dispute such as the industry-wide strike in 2000 has hastened this process further. In 2001, it culminated in a spate of mill-level disputes which, given the generally strained nature of industrial relations, turned violent. Inter-union fights worsen the situation.

Again as in cotton textiles, in jute industrial relations were strained in the 1980s with a major strike in 1984. Thereafter, the threat of closure was perpetually present, or strategically used, by many vulnerable mills to extract wage concessions from workers. There was widespread disillusionment with the central trade unions. In the early-1990s, two cases of closure became highly publicized, the Kanoria Jute Mill, which was managed by a worker cooperative following closure, and the Titagurh Jute Mill, whose closure led to several cases of death and suicide. From the mid-1990s, even though the general prospect of the industry improved, costs have been highly variable due to fluctuations in jute prices and erratic power supply. Since 1998-9, the problem of cost has been especially serious. Most mills do not have the reserves to tide over these fluctuations. The import of cheap jute products from Bangladesh and collapse of the Jute Packaging Order added to the uncertainties. The outcome is extreme vulnerability. Most mills have not modernized, and carry a large labour cost as overhead. If they are to reduce costs they have to target labour.

Contract labour provides some flexibility in adjustment. Given the seasonality of jute production, there has always been an incentive to employ contract labour on the manufacturing process. Further, some mills routinely close down in summer, though each time it is technically an illegal closure. But the ever-present uncertainty over material costs means default dues to regular workers is a frequent occurrence. On top of all this, thanks to its location in the heart of West Bengal, jute has always had strained industrial relations, with or without support from the government in power. Given this combination of managerial failure, history of militancy and political backing to labour, and high price-cost uncertainty, industrial relations in jute are a perpetual powder keg.

In 2000-1, relations were especially strained, and violent incidents more frequent than usual. The incidents occurred in a number of jute mills along the east and west banks of the river Hooghly. The provocations were non-payment of wages, actual or threatened closure, attempted negotiations at voluntary retirement, inter-union fight for control, etc.

Jute needs modernization and retrenchment through negotiated means. But neither has been easy in this industry, which survives by and large for short-term profits. As for the workers, there has not been a significant change either way due to the reforms. Employment has been almost stationary. However, there has been a change in the dynamics of violence. Violence has become decentralized with the disappearance of industry-wide unions and divisions among employers.

Synthetic Textiles

Import tariffs on the major manmade fibres and raw materials were brought down, step by step, from their peak level of 185 per cent in 1991-2 to 30 per cent in 1997-8. This dealt a blow to a number of manmade fibre manufacturers. Between 1995 and 1999, world prices of polyester staple fibre and filament yarn crashed, partly due to excess supply from East Asia. The majority of the firms in India making these products saw losses from 1996. Less vulnerable were larger firms like Reliance, which commanded more assured long-term contracts. But Reliance's expansion itself put further pressure on other polyester producers. By 1996, the synthetic fibre industry had simply too much capacity located in too many units operating at an average scale lower than the world average. Between 1990 and 1996, JCT, Baroda Rayon, J.K. Synthetics, Sanghi Polyester and Garware Nylon, were among the list of man-made fibre manufacturers that came to the BIFR door.

Baroda Rayon, a medium-scale firm engaged in rayon, nylon and polyester, faced problems throughout the 1990s. By 1997, burdened by unsustainable debts it tried several revival packages that included failed attempts to sell its plants to larger producers. In 1999, its polyester unit began being operated under different management. However, the rayon unit shut down. From the end of 1999, the company began defaulting on salaries, leading to a spate of protests and rallies from its 4,500 strong workforce. The textile operations of J.K. Synthetics, the main company of the G.H. Singhania group, was another casualty of adverse market conditions. In 1997, faced with massive indebtedness (for some time, the company was the leading bad debtor among all private sector bad debtors of commercial banks), the company closed eight units in Kota and Jhalawar. The unemployment of 5,000 workers had a traumatic impact on the local economy, and numerous small firms ancillary to these plants also closed. In all these cases of closure, there was remarkably little resistance from workers. In fact, the government was explicitly non-interventionist in these cases.[31] Studies of textile mill closure in Gujarat, and press reports from Rajasthan both underscore a point highlighted in some recent assessments of trade unionism, the distinctly non-interventionist attitude of some states in respect of closure and large-scale disputes.

CONCLUSION

Manufacturing has seen six processes each one of which has taken a toll on existing jobs, whether in terms of number or quality. These are:

- Closure and industrial decline in sections of the organized sector.
- Reallocation of labour, within the organized sector between industries.
- Reallocation of labour within the organized sector between different types of job—from permanent to contractual, from tasks integrated in the firm to tasks performed on contract outside the firm, etc. This process has been called casualization and informalization.
- Reallocation of labour between organized and unorganized sectors. This process has also been called casualization and informalization, and feminization in some contexts.
- A process of general reduction in pay, or growth of pay, welfare, and job-security as a result of these processes.
- A process of general disempowerment of labour, or a loss of strength of trade unions to resist these processes.

We are now in a position to answer the questions posed at the beginning of this essay.

What has been the net effect of these processes in terms of actual job-loss? How large has job-loss been? My estimates suggest that the overall extent of job-loss in the organized sector has been very limited in the 1990s. In the peak period of the reforms, gross jobs lost were by far outweighed by gross jobs created. In fact, job-loss has been both sectorally and temporally concentrated, which shows that the reforms as such has had rather little adverse impact. Three sectors, all in textiles, account for the bulk of job-loss. Except man-made fibre textiles, where the reforms played a direct role, in cotton and jute the reforms did not create the crisis for labour. The crisis had old roots. However, the disempowerment effect of the reforms did play a role in making conditions harder for labour in these sectors. Not policy directly, but politics and mentality change made closure and retrenchment easier in crisis-ridden industries. In cotton textiles, there was large-scale outright retrenchment. In jute textiles, there was a significant increase in violent disputes.

To sum up, the reforms have made things worse. But it did not make things as bad as one might think. The really worst hit sectors had old problems. In these sectors and elsewhere, implicit changes in labour regime played a bigger role. It is a plausible hypothesis that it was the increase in flexibility in the market through the informal route that softened the negative impact of the reforms. Disempowerment and job-loss have been negatively correlated during the 1990s.

How far has reallocation of labour from declining to profitable sectors happened? We have seen that there are strong reasons to believe that reallocation both within and between sectors have been quite significant. Reallocation may have played an especially important role in the current recession.

What role has labour market institutions played in the whole transition? Generally, the disempowerment effect upon organized labour has played a key role in labour market adjustments, both in declining industries and in profitable ones. This is significant precisely because formally so little has happened in terms of labour reform.

NOTES

1. I wish to thank other members of the team, including and especially Shuji Uchikawa, for comments and suggestions. In addition, responses to some of the findings, received from S.P. Kashyap, Rakesh Basant, Sebastian Morris, Amita Shah, and Uma Rani, are gratefully acknowledged.

2. For example, . . . *and our rice pots are empty: The Social Cost of the Economic Crisis*, Consumer International, London, 1998.
3. The term 'distributional coalition', a group that in effect tries to capture a larger share of the common product without necessarily contributing to the size of the common product, owes to Mancur Olson, *The Rise and Decline of Nations. Economic Growth, Inflation, and Social Rigidities*, Yale University Press, New Haven, 1982. *Weapons of the Weak* is the title of a book on peasant resistance, by the anthropologist James Scott.
4. S. Mundle, 'Structural Adjustment, Employment and Redundancy in Organized Sector in India', in R. Islam (ed.), *Social Dimensions of Economic Reforms in Asia*, New Delhi: ILO-ARTEP, 1994; I.Z. Bhatty, 'Protective Net for Workers in an Exit Policy: A Proposal', National Council of Applied Economic Research Working Paper No. 42, New Delhi, 1993.
5. ILO, *Economic Reforms and Labour Policies in India*, New Delhi, 1996.
6. If the estimation is done yearwise, that is, if L is compared for successive pairs of dates like 1980-90, 1980-91, 1980-92, etc., the L often comes out as negative for individual years, which cannot be interpreted except as an underestimation in jobs created.
7. *Business Standard*, 11 October 1997.
8. For a selection of writings, I.J. Ahluwalia, *Productivity and Growth in Indian Manufacturing*, Oxford University Press, Delhi, 1991; Ajit Ghose, 'Economic Restructuring, Employment and Safety Nets', ILO-ARTEP, *Social Dimensions of Structural Adjustment in India*, ILO, Delhi, 1995; R. Nagraj, 'Employment and Growth in Manufacturing Industries: Trends, Hypotheses and Evidence', *Economic and Political Weekly*, 29(4), 27 January 1994; S.R. Bhalotra, 'The Puzzle of Jobless Growth in Indian Manufacturing', *Oxford Bulletin of Economics and Statistics*, 60(1), 1998; K.V. Ramaswamy, 'The Search for Flexibility in Indian Manufacturing: New Evidence on Outsourcing Activities', *Economic and Political Weekly*, 34, 6-12 February 1999; and B.N. Goldar, 'Employment Growth in Organized Manufacturing Growth in India', *Economic and Political Weekly*, 35(14), 1 April 2000.
9. Deepita Chakravarty, 'Labour Market under Trade Liberalisation in India. Some Issues Concerning Reallocation', *Economic and Political Weekly*, 27 November 1999.
10. Chakravarty, 'Labour Market'.
11. S. Gangopadhyay and W. Wadhwa, 'Economic Reforms and Labour', *Economic and Political Weekly*, 22, 1998.
12. Jeemol Unni, in a survey of South Asian employment data until the early-1990s, shows that there is clear evidence that in the 1980s and the early-1990s, 'feminization' and informalization of the non-agricultural workforce took place. See 'Gender and Informality in the Labour Market in South Asia', Gujarat Institute of Development Research Working Paper No. 117, Ahmedabad, 2000.
13. For a discussion of the regime, see ILO, *Economic Reforms and Labour Policies in India*.
14. T.C.A. Anant, S. Gangopadhyay and O. Goswamy, 'Industrial Sickness in India', Report 1, New Delhi, 1992, mimeo.
15. *Business Standard*, 16 November 1999.
16. *Business Standard*, 1 May and 13 June 1998.

17. See, for a review, Mrinal Datta Chaudhuri, 'Labor Markets as Social Institutions in India', IRIS-India Working Paper No. 10, University of Maryland at College Park, Maryland (MD), 1996.
18. ILO, *Economic Reforms and Labour Policies in India.*
19. These terms were introduced by W. Sengenberger and Frank Pyke, see for a discussion, M. Holmstrom, 'Employment in Smaller Indian Firms. Choices under Liberalisation', *Economic and Political Weekly*, Review of Labour, 25 September 1999. The essay discusses alternatives to the low and high roads, which include strengthening various types of collective institutions in small firms.
20. See, for example, Pradeep Agrawal, 'Labour Policies, Employment and Worker Earnings: Indian and International Experiences', IRIS-India Working Paper No. 20, University of Maryland, MD, 1996.
21. For a discussion of cases, see Christopher Candland, 'Labor Institutions and Industrial Restructuring in India', IRIS-India Working Paper No. 24, University of Maryland, MD, 1996; Ernesto Noronha, 'Liberalisation and Industrial Relations', *Economic and Political Weekly*, 24 February 1996.
22. For figures on the rise in the extent of contracting in the organized sector, see the essays by Shuji Uchikawa and K.V. Ramaswammy in this volume. For a recent newspaper report on official reactions to contracting, see 'Outsourcing worries labour minister', by Saibal Dasgupta, *Business Standard*, 14 August 1998.
23. I borrow 'off-loading' from Kavaljit Singh and Nilanjan Mukhopadhyay, 'Globalization and India: The Other Side of "Success": Bayer in India', Public Interest Research Group, Delhi, 2001.
24. See, for an overview, Dabashish Bhattacharjee, 'Globalising Economy, Localising Labour', *Economic and Political Weekly*, 14 October 2000.
25. See, for a discussion of the literature, Candland, 'Labor Institutions and Industrial Restructuring in India'.
26. Suchita Kulkarni, 'Impact of Restructuring of the Bombay Textile Industry on Labour and Labour Institutions', *Indian Journal of Labour Economics*, 42(4), 1999.
27. No direct estimate of job-loss in cotton textiles is available. This estimate is based on the following figures: workers on roll in 1995 was 1.023 million, workers employed in active factories (ASI, 1995) was 0.578 million, the difference must be in closed factories which numbered 181 in 1995. This gives us an average of 2,456 workers per closed mill, or 2,72,000 workers in 111 closed mills.
28. Supriya Roy Chowdhury, 'Industrial Restructuring, Unions and the State. Textile Mill Workers in Ahmedabad', *Economic and Political Weekly*, 24 February 1996; Jude Howell and Uma Khambhampati, 'Liberalization and Labour: The Fate of Retrenched Workers in the Cotton Textile Industry in India', *Oxford Development Studies*, 27(1), 1999; Ernesto Noronha and R.N. Sharma, 'Displaced Workers and Withering of Welfare State', *Economic and Political Weekly*, 5 June 1999; Kiran Desai, 'Workers of Closed Textile Mills: A Case of South Gujarat'; and B.B. Patel, 'Socio-economic Marginalisation of Displaced Textile Mill Workers in Ahmedabad, Gujarat, India', seminar papers for Collective Care Arrangements among Workers and Non-workers in the Informal Sector, Hyderabad, 2001.
29. For example, Roy Chowdhury, 'Industrial Restructuring'; and Howell and Khambhampati, 'Liberalization and Labour'.

30. 'West Bengal: Labour as Politics', *Economic and Political Weekly*, Editorial, 20 January 2001.
31. 'Secretary for Industries N.S. Sisodia, does not dispute [that the closure was a result of liberalization], saying it could be a possible reason but then, he adds, no one can dispute this right of the industrialist. He, however, said it was family dispute between the Singhanias which led to the crisis. . . . The workers are blaming every political party here for letting them down as none took up their cause.' Quoted in Rajesh Sinha, 'Units Closing in on the Life of Rajasthan', *The Indian Express Online*, 3 December 1997.

Liberalization, Outsourcing and Industrial Labour Markets in India: Some Preliminary Results

K.V. RAMASWAMY[1]

1. INTRODUCTION

Labour market outcomes play a crucial role in the evaluation of industrial and trade liberalization policies. Initial resistance and the observed opposition to liberalization spring from perceived adverse effects in terms of employment and wages. Given the conditions of labour supply, the labour market outcomes are a consequence of changes in demand, technology and competitive conditions in the product markets. The competitive environment of Indian industrial firms has changed following the liberalization of industrial and trade policies in the nineties. Management of industrial firms responded to these changes by initiating a process of restructuring their operations. What has been the impact of these changes on the industrial labour markets? This paper focuses attention on one important channel of transmission namely, outsourcing practices. The outsourcing of production workers, services, final products and components reflects the *distancing* strategies, particularly in the presence of dual labour markets, on the part of industrial firms to gain new margins of flexibility in increasingly competitive markets. For analytical purposes two different perspectives on the relationship between labour market outcomes and product market conditions in the period of economic reforms can be identified. One view is that restructuring and technology orientation would lead to a decline in employment growth in organized industry and workers would crowd into unorganized sector with low productivity and real wages. Greater outsourcing of labour intensive products could cause a decline in formal well-paid employment. Linkages may weaken due to removal of capacity restrictions on the large-scale sector further reducing output demand and employment in informal sector enterprises.[2] An alternative view could be formulated as follows. The direction of change in employment elasticity of output in organized industry could go either way depending on the factor-intensity bias of technological change and the output mix change. Capacity restriction is just one of the several factors driving subcontracting practices. Saving of wage and non-wage benefits of formal employment is not always the primary reason for outsourcing by firms in the organized sector. Broadly speaking outsourcing is the result of a change in the cost boundaries facing firms as they choose between 'make or buy' decisions. Several factors are at work and what happens to labour market outcomes is an empirical matter. Following this perspective[3] this paper will make a preliminary attempt to investigate the association between subcontracting practices and labour market outcomes during the period of economic reform. Towards this objective we adopt the following approach. First we document the extent of subcontracting activity in Indian manufacturing industries. Second we observe the patterns of outsourcing/subcontracting intensity of industries in the registered manufacturing sector. Third, study the behaviour of employment, labour productivity and real wages of contract- intensive industries relative to others. We arrive at certain tentative conclusions in the light of aggregate employment and output performance of the Indian manufacturing during the reform years. In this paper we will be using the terms 'outsourcing' and 'subcontracting' interchangeably.

This paper is organized as follows. Following this introduction, in section 2 we look at the selected aggregate statistics on manufacturing employment, casual labour and real wages to provide the background. Section 3 contains a digression on the concept of subcontracting and discusses the impact of industrial policy under the planning period on the subcontracting practices in Indian manufacturing. It outlines the possible labour market outcomes as a consequence of liberalization and its impact on subcontracting. Section 4 introduces the index of subcontracting intensity and the problems of measurement. Our estimates of the index for the manufacturing sector and for the selected industry groups are presented. Section 5 is the core of the paper and attempts to relate contract intensity with labour market outcomes in terms of earnings differentials and employment. Section 6 contains the concluding remarks.

2. MANUFACTURING EMPLOYMENT, USE OF CASUAL LABOUR, LABOUR PRODUCTIVITY GROWTH AND REAL WAGES: THE AGGREGATE SCENARIO

The growth in GDP and hence the domestic demand during the reform period did not undergo a significant change.[4] Annual average growth rate of exports is higher in the 1990s (9.8 per cent in dollar values) than in the 1980s (8.2 per cent). On an average basis, export to GDP ratio increased from 5.0 per cent in the 1980s to 9.8 per cent in the 1990s (RBI, 1999). Manufacturing employment recorded a growth rate of 1.7 per cent per annum during the reform years of the 1990s as shown in Table 1. The growth rate will be higher if one includes employment in repair services, which has grown rapidly.[5] This is a turnaround change relative to the 1980s when employment in total manufacturing had declined in absolute numbers (Table 2). Employment in registered factories had grown at 0.6 per cent between 1981 and 1991.[6] The 1990s show a growth rate of 0.5 per cent in factory employment indicating the continuing slow rate of absorption by the organized manufacturing sector. Within the factory sector, the use of casual labour did not show substantial change in the period of liberalization. Microeconomic studies had documented the widespread use of market mediated work practices and outsourcing of labour long before economic reforms were initiated.[7] It includes greater use of contract, temporary and casual workers, and on-site labour only subcontracting. In the aggregate the use of contract labour has risen from 12 per cent in 1985-6 to 16 per cent in 1997-8. This is consistent

TABLE 1. MANUFACTURING EMPLOYMENT GROWTH

(in millions)

	1993-4	*1999-00*	*Growth Rate**
Factory	7.7	7.9	0.5
Non-Factory	32.3	36.3	2.0
Total	40.0	44.2	1.7
Urban	19.2	21.2	1.7
Rural	20.5	22.5	1.6

NOTE: * Annual Compound Growth Rate.
Here Manufacturing Excludes Repairs, Electricity, Gas and Water.

SOURCE: Author's Estimates based on Sundaram (2001a and 2001b) and *Annual Survey of Industries, Summary Results for the Factory sector,* various years.

TABLE 2. EMPLOYMENT IN MANUFACTURING AND REPAIR SERVICES

(in millions)

	1984-5	*1989-90*	*1994-5*
Factory Sector	7.05	7.31	8.17
Non-Factory	36.95	35.47	33.20
Total	44.00	42.78	41.37

SOURCE: Statement 4 in Kulshreshta and Singh (2001) and ASI Factory Sector Summary Results 1984-5, 1989-90 and 1994-5.

with the reported trend towards labour contracting for non-core activities like cleaning and maintenance, packaging, welding, painting and warehouse activities.[8] This represents one facet of management response to changing market conditions.

Our estimates in Table 1 suggest that the unorganized sector is a significant contributor to employment growth. The earlier trend of absolute declines seems to have been reversed.[9] Growth in three important segments of unorganized manufacturing in the 1990s, namely, own-account enterprises (OAME), non-directory establishments (NDME) and directory manufacturing establishments (DME) are not known. It must await the availability of disaggregated results from the 55th NSS employment surveys for the year 1999-00. We can only note that trends for the period 1989-94 (Lalitha 2000). Two segments experienced positive employment growth, namely, *urban* establishments with less than five workers (NDMEs) and establishments with more than six workers with at least one hired worker (DMEs). Between 1989-94, employment in urban NDMEs grew at 1.3 per cent and at 0.7 per cent in urban DMEs. However, total unorganized employment in manufacturing declined at the rate of 1.3 per cent per annum between 1989 and 94.

The average worker productivity in the Indian economy is estimated to have risen at the rate of 5.5 per cent per annum during the period 1994-2000. And the average annual wage earnings per worker have grown at above 3 per cent (Sundaram 2001a). Our estimate of worker productivity in total manufacturing is slightly above 4 per cent. However, worker productivity in organized manufacturing has risen at a faster rate (5.4 per cent) than in unorganized manufacturing (at about 3 per cent). More interestingly, our estimates show that between 1989-94, the real earnings per worker in the factory sector have risen only by about 0.8 per cent. In contrast, earnings in unorganized

TABLE 3. REAL EARNINGS PER WORKER IN UNORGANIZED MANUFACTURING

	1989-90	*1994-5*	*Growth Rate**
Urban-DME	3,846.8	4,683.5	4.0
Rural-DME	1,418.5	1,989.6	7.0
Urban-NDME	2,206.9	3,634.8	10.5
Rural-NDME	1,365.0	2,314.7	11.1
Factory**	10,045.0	10,464.0	0.8

NOTES: * Annual Compound Growth Rate.
Earnings in rupees adjusted using CPI for Industrial Workers with base 1982 = 100.
** Manufacturing excluding Repairs, Electricity and Gas.

SOURCE: Author's estimates based on NSSO (1995) and CSO, *Annual Survey of Industries*, various years

TABLE 3.1. GROWTH OF REAL EARNINGS IN UNORGANIZED MANUFACTURING: 1995-2000

Segment	*1994-5*	*1999-2000*	*Growth rate*
Urban Establishments	4,169.5 (11,633)	4,961.5 (21,235)	3.5
Rural Establishments	2,129.4 (5,941)	3,159.8 (13,524)	8.2

NOTE: Annual earnings in rupees. Figures in brackets are nominal earnings.
SOURCE: NSSO, 1998 and 2001.

manufacturing have risen at a faster rate[10] as shown in Table 3 and Table 3.1. This aggregate trend suggests that the earnings differentials between formal factory and the 'informal' sector earnings are unlikely to have widened in the years of liberalization. It is in this context we ask the question what has been the trend in employment, earnings and productivity in 'contract intensive', to be defined below, industries.

3. OUTSOURCING, INDUSTRIAL POLICY AND LABOUR MARKETS

3.1. Subcontracting: Concepts

We define the term subcontracting to mean the manufacture of goods by one firm for another based on latter's specifications (Lazerson 1990). This differs from a narrower UNIDO (1974) definition that states

> . . . a subcontracting relationship exists when a firm (the principal) places an order with another firm (the subcontractor) for manufacture of parts, components, subassemblies or assemblies to be incorporated into a product which the principal will sell. Such orders may include the treatment, processing or finishing of materials or parts by the subcontractor at the principals request.[11]

Our definition encompasses transactions where the principal firm places an order either for the whole product or parts of the product, which it either sells directly to the consumer or incorporates into the product that it manufactures. Contract manufacturing perhaps correctly captures the nature of the transaction. Two main forms of subcontracting are commercial and industrial subcontracting. In commercial subcontracting the role of the principal firm is limited to marketing and distributing the subcontractors finished product. The principal firm itself may not be engaged in the manufacture of that product.

The essence of subcontracting is that one or more firms must mediate the relationship between the subcontractor and the final user of the product/end market.[12] The existing literature tends to focus on vertical inter-firm relationships and in particular between small and large firms (well known is the one between small component suppliers and automobile manufacturers). Vertical inter-firm links are essentially specialized contracting relationships. Equally important and of recent origin is the horizontal subcontracting that takes place between two firms operating at the same horizontal stage of the vertical chain of production. This is not confined to small-large variety. Two large (even rival) firms are found to engage in subcontracting arrangements. For example, Videocon supplying Power Wash machines to Godrej-GE. Suppliers of refrigerators, electric fans, thermoware, steel furniture and domestic electric appliances constitute the numerous instances of horizontal subcontracting between large and small firms. Capacity subcontracting is horizontal in nature.[13] Demand uncertainty due to cyclical or seasonal variations in demand is known to encourage capacity subcontracting by large firms. Current demand in excess of installed capacity would be met by outsourcing from the sub-contractors. Small firms are known to function as a buffer to cyclical fluctuation of industry demand. Firms in the organized sector are reported to shift the transitory demand for their products to unorganized manufacturing.[14]

3.2 Industrial Policy and Subcontracting

Outsourcing of products, services and labour have been widely practised by Indian industrial firms long before the reform years. Segmented labour markets divided into formal and informal segments is supposed to be a major determinant of outsourcing of product as well as labour. Formal sector employment is well paid, governed by long-term contract, subject to government regulations and trade union pressure. Informal segment is outside the job security regulations, pays lower wages, free from union wage agreements, and escapes government regulations on health and safety. Subcontracting is reported to be the typical response of large unionized firms in India. To quote 'The farming out is so extensive in some cases that the firm's own employees have been reduced to a fraction of it's total employment, and the character of the firm itself transformed from a manufacturing to a trading one. State policies restricted the growth of large domestic firms and firms with foreign equity.'[15] At the same time State policy encouraged small-scale factories through product reservation and other promotional measures like concessional credit for fixed and working capital, preferential purchase by public sector enterprises and fiscal incentives. Small-scale sector was not subjected to capacity licensing. A large number of products were reserved exclusively for small-scale producers and large firms were not allowed entry into those product lines. The industrial policy did permit setting up of capacity by large firms if it were for internal consumption. This had the effect of forcing firms to invest in capacities that otherwise they would have outsourced. The policy of protection through reservation forced large firms with frozen capacities to outsource additional output. The promotional policies facilitated outsourcing by creating a small-scale sector capable of producing numerous intermediate and final products with simple technology. Small firms mostly obtained the technology from their customer firms and equipment suppliers.[16] The scrutiny of annual reports of large business houses and foreign equity companies revealed ownership of plants in the small-scale sector.[17] Exemption from payment of excise tax has been the most attractive fiscal incentive for small firms. The value of this incentive scheme is found to be very high as rates of duty varied from 15 per cent to 105 per cent. Most of these policies and the market conditions changed during the reform period. The impact of fiscal policy reforms in terms of reduction of excise duty differentials and the manufacturing value added tax (VAT) is not clear.

3.3 Liberalization, Subcontracting and Labour Markets

Why and what way outsourcing activity can be expected to undergo change following liberalization in the nineties? What are the observed effects and constraints? First, liberalization increases product market competition and competitive pressure forces firms to achieve efficiency in the organization of production. This is expected to increase outsourcing. Entry of foreign multinational companies, direct import competition due to tariff reduction and the relaxation of capacity licensing and expansion restrictions on large domestic companies did led to an intensification of the degree effective competition across product groups. Management of industrial firms responded to these changes by initiating a process of restructuring their operations. In particular the effort has been on shedding marginal activities and focusing on core competencies. Regulatory regime of the planning period had the effect of excessive integration and overdiversification. Second, an open trade regime is expected to favour labour-intensive manufactured exports. Contract manufacturing is pervasive in export activity. Both multinational and domestic firms are expected to increase outsourcing for exports. Third, greater domestic and import competition would bring about changes in corporate strategies in terms of increased product differentiation and niche markets. This would create greater scope for outsourcing by putting a premium on the ability to meet unanticipated demand. Fourth, industrial firms in an economy in transition to market-oriented and global competition is likely to face greater technological uncertainty. Faced with technological uncertainty, firms will avoid the risk of making large investments in soon-to-be obsolete technologies by relying on market provision of those products (or buy decision instead of make). Market liberalization can unleash forces that favour integrated production and reduce the scope for outsourcing. Relaxation of capacity restrictions on the large firms and technological upgradation of downstream firms are the two important factors.[18] This would cause reduction of labour demand in upstream firms and contribute to negative labour market outcomes. Outsourcing of products is not driven solely by wage differentials between formal and informal employment. Other significant factors at work are the strategic need for core competencies, search for flexibility advantages in fragmented product markets and the need for specialized services. The labour market consequences in terms of wage differentials and employment growth is an empirical matter.

4. ESTIMATES OF PRODUCT OUTSOURCING: FACTORY SECTOR

4.1 Measurement and Data

The balance sheets of companies do not report the value of products produced in-house during the year and that is bought out separately. We need separate data on components/products bought out and incorporated in the company's final product and that product which is bought out but sold directly to the final consumer perhaps after stamping the company's brand name. The most widely used data on industries in India is the Annual Survey of Industries (ASI). The ASI is based on data collected from factories, under the Factories Act 1948, with more than 10 workers.[19] The Census sector of ASI covers factories with 50 workers and above using power and those with above 100 workers without power. Data in somewhat greater detail is available at 3-digit level of National Industrial Classification (NIC) for selected years. The ASI data presents estimates of value added by subtracting the gross value of inputs from the gross value of output. From our viewpoint the following two categories deserve attention. First, sale value of goods sold in the same condition as purchased. Second, contract and commission work done by others on materials supplied. We believe that data on these two types of transactions may be regarded as significant measures of subcontracting activity of factories in the registered sector. The first transaction is suggested to capture trading activity of small firms.[20] For registered factories, subject to auditing, we believe that it does not stand for trading transaction.[21] Consider the following two examples: Factory G purchases finished steel book-racks from an informal sector factory and sells it as its own, after stamping its brand name. The same factory also buys rolled steel as input but sells to another factory. The second example is a clear case of trading activity but under the sales tax provision cannot be shown as sales revenue. We argue that reported data on 'Sale value of goods sold in the same condition as purchased' essentially captures the transaction indicated by the first example. Industrial firms also supply raw materials to other factories for treatment, finishing and processing. This is one form of traditional putting-out production in which the firm chooses the labour-intensive activity for outwork. Data on the value of work done by other concerns (factories/workshops) on material supplied is a measure of the value of subcontracting activity. For large factories, the value of such activity constituted 5.3 per cent of value added in 1973-4. It is around 4.5 per cent in 1992-3. For the registered manufacturing sector it is estimated to be around 8 per cent in 1983-4 and 7 per cent in 1993-4.

We have taken the value of goods sold in the same condition as purchased plus the value of work done by other concerns on material supplied as a measure of the value of subcontracting. And its share in value of purchased material inputs excluding power and fuel as an index of subcontracting intensity. It measures the degree of product subcontracting in an industry. A limitation of this index requires to be stated. This does not capture the bought out components incorporated into the final product. The accounting practices would record this as purchased inputs. In this exercise we are not able to capture this type of specific vertical subcontracting activity. To this extent our index underestimates subcontracting transactions. A second limitation arises from exporting activities of small establishments. A large number of small-scale enterprises export through exporting and trading houses. That is exporters who are not manufacturers. Contract manufacturing is pervasive in export activity. We are not capturing this explicitly in our indices. However, as our broad focus is to determine the relative outsourcing intensity of industries at the aggregate level these limitations are unlikely to affect our conclusions.

4.2 Estimates of Subcontracting Intensity

Our estimates of subcontracting intensity are shown in Table 4. Subcontracting intensity in the factory sector of manufacturing has risen from 10.7 per cent to 12.3 per cent in 1994-5. The real value of subcontracting activity during this period has grown at the compound growth rate of 10.9 per cent. Subcontracting activity is growing at a faster rate than output growth rate in manufacturing.

TABLE 4. GROWTH OF OUTSOURCING IN MANUFACTURING*: 1990 TO 1995

	Factory sector 1989-90	*Factory sector 1994-5*	*Rate of growth*
Subcontracting Intensity*	10.7	12.3	
Top 100 Industries**	30.1	29.0	
Real Value of Subcontracting (Rs. crore)	7,048.0	13,092.0	10.9

NOTES: Manufacturing Excludes Repairs.
* Average of 377 industry groups.
** Ranked in terms of subcontracting intensity.
SOURCE: CSO, *Annual Survey of Industries*, various years.

We estimated the subcontracting intensity for 377 three-digit industries in 1989-90 and 1994-5. Then we selected the top 100 industries after ranking them in terms of subcontracting intensity. These top 100 industries were reclassified in terms of use-based categories, namely, basic, intermediate, consumer durable and non-durables. We did not observe any significant change in the average intensity of the use-based groups. A set of selected 3 digit industries and their contract intensities are presented in Table 5. Significant increase is observed in a number industry groups. Some of the important industries are electrostat and photocopy machines, voltage stabilizers, rain-coats and hats, electric lamps, metal furniture, rolling shutters, electric domestic appliances, ceramic ware, and surgical cotton. Higher outsourcing in photocopy machines, computer systems indicate greater assembly type manufacturing activity. Increasing localization of production by foreign owned companies is an important reason. A significant source of this increase in subcontracting is the growth in the volume of production of consumer durables. Consumer durable goods sector experienced relatively higher rates of growth in the nineties (see Ramaswamy 2001). The larger volumes enabled greater specialization of parts production. Many subcontracting firms have been set up to supply parts to consumer durables, automobiles and electrical appliances. The significant decline in outsourcing occurred in the group manufacture of clothing accessories. This is apparently an effect of the decline in export growth of garment industry in the 1990s. In our earlier analysis of data on large factories (factories with more than 200 workers) we had observed the dominance of consumer non-durables. Table 6 shows the distribution of industries by their subcontracting intensity namely, basic goods (BG),

TABLE 5. CONTRACT INTENSITY IN SELECTED INDUSTRIES

	1989-90	*1994-5*
Radiographic x-ray apparatus, tubes & parts	1,427.00	1,748.7
Accounting machines, cash registers, postage	262.90	204.1
Electrostat and photocopy machines	3.06	55.3
Voltage stabilizers	19.10	45.2
Special purpose non-electrical machinery	16.60	37.3
Computers and computer based systems	20.20	20.1
Raincoats, hats, etc. (plastic/waterproofs)	88.40	125.0
Spinning, weaving, etc., of silk other than mills	15.60	115.9
Stationery articles nec (file covers, etc.)	95.60	97.0
Weaving and finishing of cotton khadi	51.40	87.6
Weaving and finishing of synthetic fabrics (handlooms)	43.50	79.0
Other electric lamps	15.70	69.3
Manufacture of clothing accessories	66.40	47.6
Umbrellas, sun-umbrellas and parts	27.10	46.8
Furniture and fixtures primarily of metal	19.30	84.1
Rolling shutters of iron/steel	18.20	66.9
Apparatus for radio-broadcasting and television	NA	47.2
Sewing and knitting machines	9.05	33.6
Transmission apparatus for radio telephony/TV	3.30	33.6
Manufacture of steel trunks	NA	32.1
Electrical domestic appliances nec	11.03	19.0
Ceramicware for laboratories	82.90	89.9
Rubber surgical and medical equipment	0.60	86.3
Manufacture of plasters	9.50	86.2
Manufacture of surgical cotton and bandages, etc.	4.60	82.1
Mica products	7.90	48.6
Laboratory and scientific instruments	17.01	33.6
Manufacture of tin plates	8.80	29.6
Casting of metals	8.70	19.4

SOURCE: Author's estimates based on *Annual Survey of Industries*, 1989-90 and 1994-5.

capital (K), intermediate (INT), consumer durable (CD) and consumer non-durables (CND). They are consistent with our *a priori* expectations based on anecdotal and sample survey results reported in the literature. Consumer non-durables have the highest subcontracting intensity and their average labour intensity is also the highest. Basic goods represent process technology and continuous flow methods of production in contrast to consumer durables and non-durables in which batch production methods seems to be widespread.

TABLE 6. CONTRACTING INTENSITY BY USE-BASED INDUSTRY GROUPS: 1992-3

Industry	*Contracting intensity ranking*	*Labour per unit of value added*	*Value added share (per cent)*
Basic Goods	IV	0.4	33.0
Intermediate	V	0.7	9.0
Capital Goods	III	0.5	17.5
Consumer Non-durables	I	0.9	33.0
Consumer Durables	II	0.6	7.5
All Industries	31	0.5	100.0

SOURCE: Ramaswamy (1999). Estimates based on *Annual Survey of Industries,* 1992-3 (Census Sector).

5. CONTRACT INTENSITY AND LABOUR MARKET OUTCOMES

Is there a relationship between changes in contract intensity of industries in the reform period and earnings and productivity differentials? Do workers in contract-intensive industries earn less than the average worker in the unorganized sector? What has been the employment performance of contract-intensive industries during the reform period? These are important but difficult questions to answer because of insufficient data. This section reports some preliminary results.

If enterprises contract out exclusively with the objective of saving labour costs then the growth of contracting should result in greater earnings inequalities in the manufacturing sector. As data on earnings in the unorganized sector is not available at the 3-digit level of aggregation, we have confined our analysis to sixteen 2-digit industries. The estimates of contract intensities at the 3-digit level are summed to arrive at 2-digit level estimates. They are presented in columns 6 and 7 in Table 7. Out of the 18 two-digit industry groups 13 groups show an increase in subcontracting activity. The top five industries are textile products, metal products, beverages and tobacco, wool and silk products and chemical products in 1994-5. It is important to note that these five are also export-intensive industries. Leather industry is one exception that is not captured by our index. Perhaps the channel of direct selling to whole-sale traders dominate this sector.

The Table 7 also contains the estimates of growth in real earnings, in the unorganized segment of the 2-digit industry groups between

TABLE 7. GROWTH RATE OF REAL EARNINGS IN UNORGANIZED MANUFACTURING AND CONTRACT INTENSITY

Industry	*Earnings per worker*				*Contract intensity*	
	1990-5 DME-Urban	*1990-5 DME-Rural*	*1990-5 NDME-Rural*	*1990-5 NDME-Urban*	*1989-90*	*1994-5*
Textile products	0.4	7.7	9.8	14.0	42.4	37.9
Metal products	4.2	26.2	10.0	10.3	15.6	19.9
Bev. tobacco	2.0	3.1	29.1	10.5	32.3	19.4
Wool/silk	5.7	10.4	15.0	2.5	15.5	18.5
Chemical	-0.3	7.9	5.7	4.2	13.0	17.2
Machinery	0.4	9.4	4.2	9.4	14.1	15.6
Basic metal	1.3	-2.5	4.8	10.8	8.7	13.1
Others	9.1	-9.9	7.0	5.8	19.7	12.2
Wood	4.7	15.9	13.5	11.2	15.9	11.8
Leather	4.4	-3.3	16.2	10.4	10.0	11.3
Food	NE	-3.8	NE	NE	8.3	11.5
Cotton textiles	6.5	1.2	15.1	11.2	6.5	9.6
Jute	-0.2	1.5	24.5	5.1	5.8	7.7
Food	NE	-4.0	NE	NE	6.1	7.5
Non-metallic	2.2	–5.4	24.3	7.7	4.6	7.4
Transport	0.6	0.0	2.0	9.9	8.2	7.3
Paper	1.8	12.4	0.7	9.3	6.0	6.4
Petro and plastic products	3.4	3.1	6.4	8.0	3.1	4.2
Manufacturing	2.5	2.1	9.2	8.7	10.3	12.3

SOURCE: Estimates based on NSSO (1998) and *Annual Survey of Industries, Summary Results for the Factory Sector*, various years.

1990 and 1995. None of the top five industries have experienced decline in real earnings. There are two exceptions, namely, urban DME in the chemicals industry and rural DME in the leather industry.

Has there been an increase in the earnings differential between the organized industry and the unorganized sector in contract-intensive industries? It has been observed that the DME segment of the unorganized sector has a commodity composition similar to the factory sector (Shaw 2000). This is suggestive, in a restricted way, of greater scope for linkage between the two segments. The estimates of earnings and labour productivity differential between the formal sector (measured by ASI factory) and the urban informal sector (measured by DME urban segment) are shown in Table 8. There is no evidence of widening of real earnings differentials during the reform period. Among the contract-intensive industries two industry groups seem to

TABLE 8. EARNINGS AND PRODUCTIVITY DIFFERENTIALS: URBAN INFORMAL AND FORMAL SECTORS

(%)

	Earnings per worker			*Labour productivity differentials*		
Industry	*1984-5*	*1989-90*	*1994-5*	*1984-5*	*1989-90*	*1994-5*
Food	47.5	81.5	49.4	49.2	52.2	44.3
Beverages	71.4	58.8	50.6	54.1	21.3	22.7
Cotton textiles	24.6	27.6	34.5	27.1	18.9	23.7
Wool and silk	29.6	34.7	38.1	30.7	19.5	10.8
Jute	23.8	15.9	13.5	80.0	31.9	15.3
Textile products	59.0	63.6	55.8	22.5	25.7	18.2
Wood	127.4	6.6	56.8	47.9	46.0	44.2
Paper	34.7	34.0	32.3	23.6	24.6	15.3
Leather	42.8	43.9	50.7	50.8	22.9	31.7
Chemicals	18.9	25.3	23.3	8.0	52.1	4.9
Rubbers	29.3	31.5	41.0	19.6	11.3	7.7
Non-metallic	25.9	35.9	28.7	11.8	12.2	27.8
Basic metals	40.8	29.7	23.6	28.9	14.2	4.8
Metal	29.8	38.4	38.9	51.4	25.5	26.5
Machinery	33.0	74.5	35.2	12.5	14.8	17.7
Transport	26.4	28.1	26.3	45.4	26.3	26.7
Other manufacturing	36.2	38.6	49.4	19.7	17.8	15.6
All manufacturing	32.4	35.1	38.8	25.0	17.0	14.0

NOTE: Numbers in the table measure the earnings and productivity in the informal sector as a percentage of that in the formal (ASI Factory) sector.

SOURCE: *Annual Survey of Industries, Summary Results for the Factory Sector*, various years and NSSO establishment survey results.

experience widening of earnings. They are textile product and beverages and tobacco. Interestingly the contract intensity of both the industry groups also declined in the same period (Table 7). Greater outsourcing does not seem to increase earnings inequalities within industries.

This encouraging trend needs to be balanced by the fact that absolute earnings per worker in current prices in contract-intensive industries is not necessarily above the industry average.[22] The data for the year 1994-5 is shown in Table 9. No systematic association between contract intensity and real earnings below the sector average earnings could be observed.

In Table 10 the percentage growth in the number of enterprises and employment in the contract-intensive industries in unorganized manufacturing is presented. The employment growth in contract-

TABLE 9. EARNINGS PER WORKER IN UNORGANIZED SECTOR BY INDUSTRY: 1994-5

Industry	*Urban-DME*	*Urban-NDME*	*Urban-OAME*	*Rural-DME*	*Rural-NDME*	*Rural-OAME*
Textile products	11,781	12,100	3,671	7,440	4,871	4,262
Metal products	13,164	10,394	7,665	7,703	7,023	4,674
Beverages and tobacco	7,363	7,070	5,592	5,966	13,472	425
Wool/silk	14,485	12,534	2,168	8,590	5,413	947
Chemical	9,851	8,151	734	5,370	7,214	173
Machinery	15,016	13,088	7,072	10,820	6,042	6,457.5
Basic metal	13,394	12,013	15,873	15,852	6,240	NE
Others	18,796	9,461	4,319	12,648	6,460	6,301
Wood	11,387	10,512	7,211	6,039	7,962	1,499
Leather	11,415	8,674	3,487	10,264	7,057	726
Food	11,338	10,450	5,448	2,956	4,854	822
Cotton textiles	11,304	10,984	2,220	8,215	7,074	5,560
Jute	4,764	5,491	NE	5,107	4,395	NE
Food	9,324	8,869	4,939	3,837	5,946	3,522
Non-metallic	8,330	8,197	5,288	5,282	7,679	861
Transport	13,349	12,826	14,692	10,709	6,591	1,205
Paper	12,783	10,781	4,565	4,340	6,504	0
Plastic	13,626	10,528	10,756	9,070	8,570	0
All manufacturing*	13,067	10,141	NE	5,551	6,458	NE

NOTE: * Weighted average. Weights are employment shares.
SOURCE: Author's estimates based on NSSO (1998).

TABLE 10. EMPLOYMENT GROWTH IN CONTRACT-INTENSIVE INDUSTRIES: 1990-5

Industry	*Enterprise growth*	*Employment growth*
Textile products	-1.98	1.37
Metal products	0.92	2.10
Beverages and tobacco	-7.26	-5.58
Wool and silk	0.41	2.20
Chemical products	-6.11	-9.37
Machinery	NE	NE
Leather	-8.26	-1.62
Other manufacturing like stationery, watches and jewellery	6.88	5.34
Repair of capital goods	3.39	3.08
Repair services	1.86	2.20
All Industries	-2.33	-1.32

NOTE: Percentage change.
SOURCE: Lalitha (2000).

TABLE 11. GDP GROWTH IN UNREGISTERED SECTOR: 1994-9

Industry	*Growth rate*
Textile products	8.9
Metal products	7.2
Beverages and tobacco	12.3
Wool and silk	12.1
Chemical	8.4
Machinery	8.7
Basic metal	6.9
Others	5.1
Wood	3.9
Leather	3.7
Food	6.1
Cotton textiles	2.9
Jute	1.1
Food	NE
Non-metallic	11.8
Transport equipment	12.2
Paper	11.1
Plastic products	6.8
Manufacturing	7.1

SOURCE: National Accounts Statistics, 2000.

intensive industries can seen to be relatively better than the sector average. Two bad performers are beverages including tobacco and leather. More recent data is needed to come to any firm conclusion on employment performance. Data on output performance of the unregistered sector is available in national accounts statistics and it is presented in Table 11. The growth of output in the contract-intensive industries is clearly above the sector average during the post-reform period. Employment growth would have followed the same trend.

6. CONCLUDING REMARKS

In this paper we studied the impact of outsourcing practices on labour market outcomes during the period of liberalization in India. Liberalization of industrial markets and imports has had the desired effect in terms of increasing competition. The practice of subcontracting is an important channel through which product market changes affect labour markets. Significant results of our study are as follows:

- The value of subcontracting activity is growing at a faster rate than growth rate of output in organized manufacturing during the nineties. Large inter-industry difference in contract intensity change was observed.
- Many new industry groups have emerged with higher levels of contract intensity. Some of the important industries are electro stat and photocopy machines, voltage stabilizers, rain coats and hats, electric lamps, metal furniture, rolling shutters, electric domestic appliances, ceramic ware, and surgical cotton. Higher outsourcing in photocopy machines, computer systems indicate greater assembly type manufacturing activity. Localization of production by foreign owned companies could be an important factor. Higher growth in the volume of production in the consumer durable goods sector is another significant reason enabling specialization subcontracting.
- The top five 2-digit industries are textile products, metal products, beverages and tobacco, wool and silk products and chemical products in 1994-95. It is important to note that theses five are also export intensive industries. We did not find evidence to support the hypothesis that liberalization and the modernization reduces the value of outsourced output by large-scale organized industry.
- There is no evidence of widening of real earnings differentials during the reform period in the aggregate manufacturing. No systematic association is observed between subcontracting intensity and real earnings inequalities within industries.

The evidence that we mustered in this paper does not seem to suggest negative labour market outcomes in terms of widening earnings differentials, growth of real earnings and employment in contract intensive industries. Subcontracting would continue to be an important strategy of industrial firms. It is also a major source of flexibility. The observed large inter-industry difference in subcontracting intensity is consistent with the expectation of industrial restructuring in response to policy reform. Substantially higher rate of economic growth than that achieved in the nineties is the necessary condition to prevent the possibility of negative labour market outcomes.

NOTES

1. I wish to thank other members of the project team and the participants of the workshop on this project held at Gujarat Institute of Development Research, Ahmedabad, in January 2002 for their suggestions and support. Special thanks are due to Shuji Uchikawa for his valuable comments and encouragement. The usual disclaimers apply.
2. See for example Kundu (1993) among many others, who have expressed somewhat similar views.
3. This does not undermine in anyway the earlier argument.
4. There is some problem of comparison. This is true when GDP is measured in 1980-1 prices. GDP in 1993-4 prices for the 1980s is not available. However, it is unlikely to be different. See RBI (1999) for some discussion.
5. Separate figures only for manufacturing repairs in the new national industrial classification are not available. Factory sector data shows rapid growth of 3.3 per cent for the category 97 according to National Industrial Classification 1987.
6. Those registered under the Factories Act 1948. This is applicable to establishments with more than 9 workers using power and more than 20 if not using power.
7. Bhutan (1985) and Ramaswamy (1988). Nagaraj (1984) presents a descriptive survey.
8. The growth in casual labour in large factories is attributed to the rigidity of regulations governing factory employment. Industrial Disputes Act (IDA, 1976) stipulated that factories with more than 300 workers are required to take permission from the government before retrenching workers. The amendment to IDA in 1982 required all factories with more than 100 workers to take permission from the respective State governments before laying-off or close the factories.
9. This conclusion is based on the employment figures derived using the residual method. NSS 55th round estimates of informal sector manufacturing indicate a lower figure of 29.6 million in manufacturing. Estimate of informal sector employment in repair services is not available as they are combined with trading activity in the new national industrial classification 1998. Employment in repair of capital goods is also not available. We have not attempted to reconcile these estimates. However, the estimated GDP growth rate of 7.1 per cent in unorganized sector during 1994-9 (see Table 11 in the text) suggests that the decline in absolute employment is unlikely to have taken place. This aspect needs more data and research.
10. This is based on estimates of earnings for hired and paid workers given in Report 434 of NSSO (1998) and NSSO (2001).
11. Cited in Productivity, vol. 35, 1995.
12. See Lazerson (1990) and Holmes (1986) for further discussion.
13. It is possible to distinguish a number of *subspecies* of subcontracting arrangements between firms. In Japan subcontractors of the various automobile manufacturers are organized into tiers, with lower tier subcontractors supplying higher tier subcontractors. It is argued that in response to changing market conditions subcontracting have emerged as an alternative strategy to vertically integrated production in developed countries.

14. See Banerjee (1988) for an example from electric fan industry.
15. Under MRTP and FERA acts.
16. Desai and Taneja (1991).
17. Goyal, Rao and Kumar (1984).
18. Modernization and technology up gradation of large-scale firms require modernization of component suppliers and if this does not take place then small-scale suppliers with obsolete technology will be adversely affected.
19. Factories with 10 workers with power and factories with 20 workers without power.
20. Goldar (1988).
21. Sale of excess stock do take place but it is not equivalent to trade in intermediate inputs.
22. In some cases wages may be just enough to cover subsistence wage or poverty line wage. We have not investigated this aspect.

REFERENCES

Abraham, G. Katharine and Taylor K. Susan, 1996, 'Firm's Use of Outside Contractors: Theory and Evidence', *Journal of Labor Economics*, vol. 14, July, pp. 394-424.

Bhushan, Bharat, 1984, 'Ancillarisation: A new production Strategy', *Business India*, New Delhi, 16-29 January.

Business India, 12-25 September 1994.

Chaudhari, Mrinal Datta, 1996, 'Labor Markets as Social Institutions in India', IRIS-India Working Paper No. 10, University of Maryland at College Park, Maryland.

Banerjee, Nirmala, 1988, 'Small and Large Units: Symbiosis or Matsyanyaya', in G.K. Suri (ed.), *Small Scale Entrerprises in Industrial Development*: The Indian Experience, Sage Publications, New Delhi.

Desai, Ashok, 1985, 'Indigenous and Foreign Determinants of Technological Change in Indian Industry', *Economic and Political Weekly*, Special Number, pp. 2081-94.

Desai, A.V., Nisha Taneja, 1990, 'The Role of Small and Medium-Scale Industries in the Industrial Development of India', in *The Role of Small and Medium Scale Industries in the Industrial Development of Selected Asian Countries*, Asian Development Bank, Manila.

Goldar, Bishwanath, 1988, 'Relative Efficiency of Modern Small Scale Industries in India', in G.K. Suri (ed.), *Small Scale Entrerprises in Industrial development: The Indian Experience*, Sage Publications, New Delhi.

Goyal, S.K. et al., 1984, *Small-Scale Sector and Big Business*, Indian Institute of Public Administration, New Delhi.

Holmes, John, 1986, 'The Organization and Locational Structure of Subcontracting', in M. Storper and A.J. Scott (eds.), *Production, Work and Territory*, Allen and Unwin, London.

Kulshreshtha, A.C. and Gulab Singh, 2001, 'Informal Sector in India: Its Coverage and Contributions', in Kundu and Sharma (eds.), *Informal Sector in India: Perspectives and Policies*, Institute for Human Development, New Delhi.

Kundu, Amitabh, 1993, 'Growth and Changing Structure of Employment in Urban India: An Analysis in the Context of the New Economic Policy', *The Indian Journal of Labour Economics*, vol. 36, no. 4, October-December.

Lalitha, N., 2000, Unorganized Manufacturing Sector in the National Economy and Gujarat State: An Analysis of its Growth Dynamics and Contribution to National Income, Report No. 9, NCAER.

Lazerson, Mark, 1990, 'Subcontracting as an Alternative Organizational form to Vertically- Integrated Production', DP/20/1990, International Institute of Labour Studies, Geneva.

Nagaraj, R., 1984, 'Sub-Contracting in Indian Manufacturing Industries', *Economic and Political Weekly*, Annual Number, pp. 1425-34.

National Accounts Statistics, 2001, Central Statistical Organization, New Delhi.

National Sample Survey Organization, 1998, Unorganized Manufacturing Enterprises in India: Salient Features, Report No. 434, NSS 51st Round, New Delhi, August.

———, 1998, Unorganized Manufacturing Sector in India: Its Size, Employment and Some Key Estimates, Report No. 433, NSS 51st Round, New Delhi.

———, 2001, Informal Sector:1999-2000, Salient Features, Report No. 459, NSS 55th Round, New Delhi.

Ramaswamy, E.A., 1988, *Worker Consciousness and Trade Union Response*, Oxford University Press.

Ramaswamy, K.V., 1994, 'Small-Scale Manufacturing Industries: Some Aspects of Size, Growth and Structure', *Economic and Political Weekly*, vol. 29, 29 February, M13-23.

———, 1999, 'The Search for Flexibility in Indian Manufacturing: New Evidence on Outsourcing Activities', *Economic and Political Weekly*, vol. 34, no. 6, pp. 363-8.

———, 2002, 'Economic Reforms, Industrial Structure and Performance: the Case of Consumer Durable Goods Industry in India', in Shuji Uchikawa (ed), *Economic Reforms and Industrial Structure in India*, Manohar, New Delhi

Reserve Bank of India, 1999, Report on Currency and Finance, 1998-9.

Shaw, Amita, 2001, 'Scalar Linkages in Industries: Implications for Productivity and Employment', in Kundu and Sharma (eds.), *Informal Sector in India: Perspectives and Policies*, Institute for Human Development, New Delhi.

Sundaram, K., 2001a, 'Employment and Poverty in 1990s: Further Results from NSS 55th Round Employment-Unemployment Survey, 1999-2000', *Economic and Political Weekly*, 11-17 August, vol. 36, no. 32, pp. 3039-49

———, 2001b, 'Employment and Poverty in 1990s: A Postscript', *Economic and Political Weekly*, 25-31August, vol. 36, no. 34, p. 3326.

APPENDIX

TABLE A1. INDUSTRIES WITH HIGH SHARE OF CONTRACT LABOUR

(percentage of total workers)

Industry group	*1997-8 (Factory sector)*	*1985-6 (Factory sector)*	*1977-8 (Factory sector)*	*1986-7 (Census sector)*	*1980-1 (Census sector)*
1. Beverages and tobacco	40.3	41.6	4.3	50.9	9.1
2. Non-metallic mineral products	27.9	26.3	10.2	23.9	14.6
3. Food products	19.6	22.0	14.3	19.0	16.5
4. Basic metals	19.5	14.7	7.9	16.9	8.5
5. Wool & silk	15.4	11.4	3.8	12.5	5.5
6. Chemical products	20.2	9.7	5.9	10.2	6.8
7. Jute textiles	21.9	0.4	0.1		
All Manufacturing*	16.9	12.1	3.6	10.1	4.6

NOTE: * This Excludes Electricity, Gas and Water, Storage and Repairs.

SOURCE: Labour Bureau, Ministry of Labour, *Annual Survey of Industries, Summary Report on Absenteeism, Labour Turnover, Employment and Labour Cost*, various years and CSO, *Annual Survey of Industries, Summary Results for the Factory Sector*, 1977-78 and 1997-98.

TABLE A2. SUBCONTRACTING INTENSITY IN SELECTED INDUSTRIES (CENSUS SECTOR 1992-93)

Industry code and name	*Subcontracting intensity (percentage)*
331 Semifinished Iron & Steel Products (BG)	52.0
217 Prepared Animal Feed (INT)	112.0
234 Weaving & Finishing of Cottton Textiles on power-looms (INT)	110.0
366 TV receivers, Radio broadcasting equipment, Microphones, Record players, Cassette players, Audio & video tapes, etc. (K)	79.4
368 Electronic valves, Tubes, Capacitors, Circuits and other electronic equipment (K)	59.4
350 Agriculture Machinery and Equipment & parts (K)	37.5
335 Refrigerators, Air-conditioners & Fire fighting equipment & parts (CD)	115.0
342 Metal furnitures & fixtures (CD)	30.7
363 Electric lamps (CD)	55.4
374 Motor Vehicles & parts (CD)	17.5
387 Stationery articles (CND)	180.2
211 Vegatable oil & fats (CND)	210.0
214 Coffee & Instant Coffee (CND)	103.0
202 Canning & preparation of fruits & vegetables (CND)	178.0

265	Textile garments (CND)	32.0
304	Drugs, Medicines & Allied products (CND)	64.5
305	Cosmetics, Soaps, Detergents, Shaving products, Toothpaste and Toilet preparations (CND)	78.8

SOURCE: Ramaswamy (1999).

Contributors

R.C. DATTA is Professor, Tata Institute of Social Sciences.

SHUJI UCHIKAWA is Visiting Faculty, Indira Gandhi Institute of Development Research, and Researcher, Institute of Developing Economies-JETRO.

JEEMOL UNNI is Associate Professor, Gujarat Institute of Development Research.

ERROL D'SOUZA is Professor, Indian Institute of Management, Ahmedabad.

TIRTHANKAR ROY is Professor, Gokhale Institute of Politics and Economics.

K.V. RAMASWAMY is Associate Professor, Indian Institute of Management, Indore.

Index